Off the Wall

an anthology

by

Somewhere Else Writers

Web Page

DEDICATION

To writers around the world
who struggle with every apostrophe,
comma and semicolon; and each rhyme,
rhythm and emotion
contained in three lines or unwieldy tome,
whilst avoiding cliché, repetition and
litigation.

CONTENTS

1 *Power*   1

2 *Nature*   15

3 *Love*   27

4 *Industry*   49

5 *Fun and Games*   57

6 *Territory*   79

7 *Time*   101

8 *Grief*   117

9 *Index*   131

10 *Attributions*   134

FOREWORD

Living in Cirencester, retired and kicking my heels, I joined a local writing class under the tuition of Rona Laycock. At the end of two formal six-monthly sessions, class members were inspired to form a writers' group at a local café-bar called Somewhere Else. And so, in July 2012, the Somewhere Else Writers Group ('SEWG') was born.

'We read our work to one another, offer criticism and encouragement, share our frustrations, record our failures and successes.' This quote (taken from my introduction to the first SEWG anthology published in 2013) is not entirely accurate. The group has widened its activities to include radio broadcasts, writing workshops, and public performance, and continues to look for new ideas and opportunities. Our membership changes from time to time as people leave us for one reason or another, or new ones join. It is important, for example, to record the recent death of Richard Lutwyche, a member of the group for six years, whose calm, generous contributions are much missed.

I don't write and never have; I find it impossibly difficult. My only contribution to the group is that of a self-appointed in-house critic, in which capacity I claim no extraordinary experience or expertise. The other members graciously indulge me.

From my vantage point, I have, over the years, watched, often with near insane pride, the quality of output of individual members and watched them grow. Many have created bodies of work of extraordinary breadth and depth. This anthology is but a snapshot of their work.

I like the fact that a small local writers' group can be the birthplace of innovation, such as the use of QR codes to enable readers to listen to authors, or their designates, read their work.

Please enjoy this varied anthology, as I have.

Steven Goldblatt

Use your smart phone to read the QR Codes shown within to access the *'Somewhere Else Writers'* website and Audio links to our work, introduced and read by the author on *soundcloud.com*

1. POWER

'WHAT IT LIES IN OUR POWER TO DO,
IT LIES IN OUR POWER
NOT TO DO.'

ARISTOTLE

I Shall Have to be Punished for Writing This

Audio

'Children of the working class'
John Wieners

I do not want to write in colour,
red, purple, yellow, blue –
those shades of blood and bruises.

I do not want to write in orange –
that haunted hue of Halloween.

I must be bold, plain-speaking;
tell of prisons, beatings, blistered skin.

And so I write in black.

The blank screen glimmers
mirror-bright. I start to type.

Words, those ghosts of thoughts,
unfurl across the page.
I highlight all my text,
change the font to white.

Iris Anne Lewis

First published in Fresh Air Poetry 2019.

Universal Credit

Audio

Learn this lesson: assume the supplicant's
position, low before the arbiter.
Hang your petition on the ox's horn,
pray as it turns and plods inside the keep.
Forty-two days in the wilderness, longer
than Christ's self-chosen stay. Time to go home
and count the copper pennies in your palm, time
to scour the bins for corn cobs overlooked,
scraps on bones, nubs of bread, hide candles
and kindling, beg remission on your rent.
Time to forage hedgerows, scrape bark for baking
bread, claw the furrows for potatoes, hush
the hungry child while you lie clamped and clemmed,
fashioning hope from feathers and dung.

You may be lucky: beneficence
parsimonious may be granted
or day on day on days' delays will find you
in winter's shadow outside the castle walls.

Frank McMahon

First published in Riggwelter Poetry and in At the Storm's Edge, Palewell Press 2020.

Childhood Clips

Audio

Hailstones stored in jars
next to broken glass cakes.

Handstands in the hallway,
blood pooling in her head,
feet as cold as ice.

Under the stairs a starved meter
waiting in the dark.

Ghosts in the attic,
God and Father Christmas;
the glued up locks,
her mother's plan,
to stop them getting in.

The tunnel she dug and then filled in,
too tired to escape.

And all those nights in the garden,
reaching up,

collecting stars for ammunition.

Tina Baker

Cry of the Wolf

Snow fell the night Grandmother died. It was the time of the full moon, but only a dim light glowing through the cloud and the snowflakes spinning down in glimmering shadows hinted at its presence above the mountain forest.

Dusk was shading into night as the storm started. It was the first snow of winter. In the distance, we heard the screech of an owl and the low belling of a solitary wolf.

'The beasts will be hungry tonight,' said Grandmother. 'We must keep ourselves safe.'

She wrapped herself in her heavy cape and went outside to walk around our little house, securing the windows. She struggled with the last shutter as a gust of wind fought for possession of it, but at last, she managed to slam it shut. Only the storeroom at the back of the cottage to lock now. I heard her drop the stout wooden plank in place across the double doors. Again, came the cry of the wolf. A pack of wolves answered, howling in mournful counterpoint across the valley.

'It's going to be a rough night,' said Grandmother, as the wind rattled the roof tiles and whistled down the chimney, sending smoke wafting through the room. 'I'll give you something to help you sleep.'

As she chopped up dried herbs from the bunches hanging in the kitchen and brewed them up with the milk gently heating on the stove, the wolves kept up their chorus. They seemed to be coming nearer, but perhaps it was only the howling of the wind.

'Drink this.' Grandmother poured out the draught. I cupped the mug in my hands and took a mouthful. The milk was warm, syrupy, aromatic. I took another sip and then another. I started to drowse. Strange, she had made this drink for me often when she thought I needed soothing or when the brightness of the full moon, finding every crack in the shutters, filled the cottage with light, but I had never felt its effects so quickly. An unfamiliar lassitude overtook me, and I found it difficult to focus as I stumbled my way to bed. 'Don't worry,' she said, 'I've made it stronger than usual. It's such a wild night. It's best if you know nothing of it.'

I fell into a troubled sleep. I dreamt a wolf, its pelt shining silver-grey in the moonlight, slinked into my room and prowled around my bed before slipping away. I heard a scream. It sounded close by as though it were within the cottage, but it must have been an owl hunting prey. I tried to get up and go to Grandmother for comfort, but my limbs felt too heavy. Exhausted by the effort I sunk onto the pillows and drifted back to sleep.

The storm had subsided by the time I woke in the morning. It was no longer snowing, and the gale had blown itself out, leaving only an icy breeze in its wake. The storeroom door banged to and fro as currents of cold air caught it. Grandmother must be up. I pulled on my clothes and went to see her. There was no sign of her in the kitchen or living room. She must be in the storeroom. But it was empty, the only sign of life, the doors swinging back and fore, back and fore. I crossed the room to look out. Perhaps she was walking around the cottage to open the shutters, but the snow lay deep and untouched apart from some faint depressions the size of animal paws circling the cottage. I closed the doors and put the plank in place. For some reason, Grandmother must have opened the doors during the night. I wondered why she had done so, on such a night, in such weather, and even more puzzling, why she had not closed them when she returned indoors.

I went into her bedroom. She was lying on the bed; the blankets flung aside, her nightdress ripped. Blood had run down her face, neck and breast, staining the sheet and pillow bright red. I fetched a damp cloth and wiped away the blood as best I could. The wounds were jagged, her body cold. I needed help.

I pulled on my fur boots, thick woollen coat, hat and mittens and trudged down the snow-covered slope to the village below.

'Better hold the funeral without delay before the ground freezes,' said the old priest, shocked at the story of the wounds and torn nightgown. He crossed himself.

He arranged for Grandmother's body to be brought down to lie in the small onion-domed church. The grave diggers cleared the plot and dug the deep oblong hole before the ground hardened to iron. Three days later, the funeral was held.

There were only a few mourners at the service. Grandmother had kept her distance from the villagers, preferring the solitude of living on the edge of the forest that rose steeply above the huddled cottages on the valley floor. I had never attended school. Grandmother was a knowledgeable woman and had taught me herself. Our only contact with the village was the weekly trip to buy provisions. I recognised some of the faces, mainly women with time on their hands. *Village busybodies.* I could almost hear the scathing tones of Grandmother, as I looked at them.

One of them made the sign against the evil eye.

'Fancy wearing a scarlet hat and at her grandmother's funeral too,' I heard them whisper.

There was one face I did not recognise - a man with a silver-grey beard, smartly dressed in a fur coat, black hat and polished boots.

He stood a little apart when the body was lowered into the grave, but when the village women had dispersed, he approached me and introduced himself. He was an old friend of my grandmother, he explained, and had come to pay his last respects.

'What's your name?' he asked.

'Rosa,' I said.

'A charming name.' He put out a hand and touched my red hat. 'And so apt.' I felt hot blood flooding my cheeks. He smiled, revealing a set of perfect white teeth.

'What's your name?' I was curious. Had Grandmother ever mentioned him?

'Call me Vadim.' He smiled again. 'May I escort you home?' tucking my hand into his arm. We started the slow ascent up the track to the cottage.

He left me at the door after checking that I had food in the house and sufficient fuel for the fire. I was comforted by his concern.

'I'll come back tomorrow morning and check that you are alright. I'll help you get more provisions in. The weather looks set for snow.'

The temperature fell that night. I lay in bed shivering. In the distance, I could hear the wolves. It was as if they were singing a lament for Grandmother. At last, I drifted into sleep. I seemed to hear Grandmother's voice. *Beware the wolf. Wolves are like men. Young or old, hungry or sated, they are all the same under the pelt.*

As promised, the following morning Vadim appeared. We went down to the village, our boots crunching the ice-crusted snow.

We loaded a sledge with provisions. 'Better get plenty in,' he said. 'Bad weather is forecast. You may well be snowed in for a while.' He pulled the sledge up the hillside to the cottage. We went inside.

I unbuttoned my coat. 'Let me help you.' He stood behind me, reaching his arms over my shoulders, and grasped the heavy fabric. As he slipped the coat off, his hands brushed my newly budded breasts.

'Delightful,' he said.

The room darkened as a bank of cloud rolled down the mountain. 'I must go now, but you'll be quite safe until I return.'

It snowed for weeks. I was cut off from the village, my only company the mice scuttling behind the wainscot and the thin crows cawing as they scavenged for food. At night I heard howling as famished wolves stole nearer the village. But they did not approach the cottage. I was safe in my snowbound solitude.

Time passed slowly, measured only by the moon's waxing and waning, as my breasts flowered into fullness and my first woman's course flowed.

It was the night of the third full moon after Grandmother's death. The spring thaw had begun. Light flooded the valley as it reflected off the melting snow, illuminating the path down the mountainside. Tomorrow I would be able to reach the village.

I lay in bed, drowsing as clouds floated across the moonlit sky. The wolves were in full voice, one, in particular, howling louder than the rest. I heard Grandmother's voice, *they're all the same under the pelt.* I roused from sleep. Luminous eyes were watching me.

I looked up at the silver-grey muzzle, the open jaws, the perfect white teeth. I heard the cry of the wolf, the screech of an owl.

Iris Anne Lewis

First published in Writing Magazine 2019.

Bull Steined!

Audio

Thunder, more thunder thundered,
Thundered,
Shaking, thundered, rumbled
Steaming hot
Dribbling rage,
rage and frustration.
No gustation, gestation, digestion. Sensation.
No gusto. No guts.
Changed to stone, steined, cold stone, shadowed, heavy,
posed,
poised,
Magritte
Mid-air,
Tumbled as I took control. Grumbled. Slumbered.
Numbered. Remembered.
Control. I have control.
In the zone, not lazyzone, lazybone. Ozone, high tone,
I run on, on, alone, flown, gone
free.
Glinting silver
on a sliver of sea.

Bridget Arregger

Sanatorium

Audio

Pastel-tinted walls, pristine surfaces,
air filtered to exclude external contagion,
clear views from well-positioned windows,
prescribed diets glowing in bowls
an exercise regime scrupulously followed.

This is a place of superior knowledge
which knows how to diagnose every condition;
we can draw upon the history of dangerous pathologies,
especially those diseases of the mind
which lead to bodily disorder.
Here we provide smiling, firm instruction to work towards our
goal, the search for harmonious living.

In time the yellow smog and sandstorms will abate,
(a permitted consequence of progress)
Here your mind can dissociate and consider
from this mountain top the future. Of course
some pathogens require more rigour
and persistence to eliminate.
Our arc of history tends towards perfection
where you and they and we are all in step.

We have taken on the burden of your doubts
so you may observe how clear the dawn
and the lotus stirring with its light.

Frank McMahon

First published in The Steel Jackdaw 2021.

Grace Notes

He sat down slowly and deliberately on the wicker chair beside the bed. A wisp of vapour floated from the cup of blackcurrant tea which sat untouched on the bedside table. Silence seemed to gather from the corners of the room and hover above the counterpane. A breath of wind stirred the curtains. A thin shaft of light illuminated the brown corduroy pattern of his trousers. He breathed out slowly.

His sister Flora had briefed him before he had arrived and made him repeat it after he had unpacked.

'This is the most important part, Marcus. If you don't get it exactly right Mother will remind you about it for the rest of the day. So, ready?'

He enumerated each part of the routine, or was it a ceremony, starting with the thumb of his right hand. 'Step one: take in her fruit tea, blackcurrant or raspberry in the Mason's Ironstone cup and saucer.'

'Where does it go?'

'On her bedside table. Step two: turn on the radio, make sure it's Radio Three... Isn't it preset already?'

Flora shook her head. 'You can't be sure she hasn't fiddled with it. I once got Classic FM. Oh! You'd think I had murdered Mozart. Step three?'

Marcus resumed. 'Bring in the newspaper so that she can read the obituaries and music reviews.'

'And be prepared to answer questions or give opinions on anything she reads out.'

He looked at his sister. 'What do I know about Kurtag or Ligeti?'

'Improvise. Step four?'

'Bring in her post and make sure her portable writing tray has pen, paper and envelopes in case she wants to reply.'

'Very good. And finally?'

'When she rises, she'll have fruit and yoghurt at the kitchen table.'

'And then you can relax. Right, Marcus, I'll see you in a week's time. Thanks again for filling in for me.'

'You're welcome. Enjoy your holiday, Flora.'

'I certainly will, except I shan't know what to do in the mornings.'

The breeze rustled the curtains again and he looked up with a slight start before pulling a sheet of paper from his left-hand trouser pocket. Mother's morning routine which he had performed faultlessly.

He had brought in her tea and waited before turning on the radio. He had then left the room to collect the paper. Returning, he saw she had not moved. He touched her hand. It was cold. There was no pulse in her wrist nor when he felt her neck. No sound of breathing. No movement when he opened her eyelids. He turned off the radio. The Waldstein Sonata. She would have grumbled at that.

'Far too romantic! Who wants sentimental music?'

He lifted her right hand again, examining the strong slender fingers, slightly swollen with arthritis. Three days ago she had played two or three Bach Preludes and Fugues, nearly disguising the occasional mis-fingering with the conviction of her performance. He had liked Bach but in a cerebral way for its mathematical rigour and intricacy. Sometimes when he was teaching maths to the sixth form, he would play recordings several times over until they could discover the patterns.

He stood up, left the bedroom and went to the piano in the large living room. Shelves were full of scores. A few had been left on the piano and he picked through these. Bartók, Prokofiev, Schoenberg. How many times had she played this loud percussive music when he and his sisters were growing up?

Of course, they all had to learn to play the piano. Hours of practising scales and if you fluffed one you had to start again. 'This is E flat minor, not G sharp!' Tears. Frustration. It became a relief when she was away performing at concerts or recitals. Practice was never enforced then.

'This is how you do it!' her favourite phrase. She had the talent to master all of Bach's 48 Preludes and Fugues, a portal to the vast piano repertoire. That was the point. She had the talent. Would she have made it to the very first rank if she had not had children? He had never asked Flora or Irene if they had ever felt as he did, loved but inconveniently requiring food and clothes and baths and education.

And now she had died, quite unexpectedly. Flora had warned him she was getting a little frail, but she was still, indisputably, the mistress of the house, still vigorous. Only yesterday she had declaimed, 'I wish we lived nearer the Cotswolds then you could take me to listen to Alfred Brendel. I see he's giving a lecture on Beethoven, the last three Sonatas. He came to one of my concerts and was very complimentary. But I could never see why he liked Schubert so much!'

He walked slowly around the room and studied the many framed photographs on the walls and shelves. His mother Virginia with other musicians and conductors. Was that Daniel Barenboim? After two or three minutes he began to search for family photos, but he could find only one. His father was standing almost shyly on the right-hand side, his wife and children occupying the middle.

It was only after he had left home for university that he began to realise how much their father had been the central figure in the life of the family, playing the major role in a minor key. A calm, steady man, the main partner in the law firm, respected by all their clients in Stamford and beyond.

And affectionately remembered, his funeral had been a major local event attracting hundreds of mourners. He smiled as he recalled his mother's reaction when she learned that her husband had requested in his Will that she play his favourite Schubert Impromptu. He could imagine the wry smile on his father's face as he wrote that request. Or was it a requirement?

And now there would be Mother's funeral. Marcus began to imagine the scale of it. Former pupils, musicians, family, of course, local dignitaries, the press. He might have to cancel his holiday plans, a group cultural tour of Northern Italy. Later, there would be decisions about the future of the family home, the house of music, built not so much of bricks and stone but of scales, fugues, canons, sonatas, marches and yet more fugues.

The grandfather clock in the corner had just registered half-past eight. He supposed he ought to tell someone what had happened.

Going into the kitchen, he made himself a coffee, pouring into it a small measure of brandy.

Frank McMahon

'First published in Scribble Magazine 2018.

Biography

Why I write

'I write to capture the intensity of experiences; in protest against injustices and evils; to explore the complexities of life and living on this planet; and to celebrate the best of ourselves.'

2. NATURE

'AND ON EACH TWIG OF EVERY TREE IN THE DELL
UNCOUNTABLE CRYSTALS BOTH DARK AND BRIGHT
OF THE RAIN THAT BEGINS AGAIN.'

EDWARD THOMAS

Wordsmiths

Audio

Letters inscribed in air; branches
write the seasons and their fickle
variations, shredding coherence
as they thresh and whine, blasts and rants
of leaves and barren seed.

Gift of the wasp's gall: indelible
tales from the oak's heart and hearing;
grand hotel and shelter, shade
for transient languor. Acorn fall.
Sap retreats, slow to reticence.

Meditation under rimed sky,
the hermit's calligraphy spread
across the crystal sheet, utterance
of promise laid in autumn's scatter.

The year turns; dew-varnished beech glints
with angled light. Decipher the forest's
library: curlicues unfurling
on spring-dancing branches, stickiness
and insect hum, in April's breeze
the *Book of Kells* unscrolling.

Frank McMahon

*First published in The Curlew and then in
At the Storm's Edge, Palewell Press 2020.*

Sunset in the Golden Valley   *Audio*

Orange orb in silent splendour
Doffs its hat to dying day
Beyond the blackening hills,
While jittery swallows,
Très bavardes,
Observing all from wires hung high above the house,
Spot speckled blackbirds' young,
Lumbering awkwardly amongst the shadows,
Expectantly to seize a wandering worm,
And orange blossom heaves its heavenly scent
From some internal reservoir
To entrance us.
Solemn hollyhocks stand scarlet sentinel
Beside the gate
While woodpeckers cease their long, industrious knocking.
Briefly a bat above us dances in the gloom
And far below lone fox barks hollow
To serenade the night watch
Of the burgeoning moon,
And all is well.

Linda Dyson

Très bavardes – very talkative

Misheard Lyrics

Audio

In the tree a blackbird sings
shrill, bubbling ululations;
uncorks my human ear, which rings
to feathered modulations.
For me, no numbness – it awakes
uplifting inspiration
forget the hemlock; this song makes
my heart feel jubilation.

Not dead of night, not wing that's broken;
but morning – now the blackbird's spoken.
This bright spring song from up above
evokes the tones of courtly love:
with music phrased like sweet romance, he
turns a young (and old) man's fancy.

The ornithologists now know
(they say) the meaning of his song
I heard it on the radio
apparently, I'm wrong.
His lyrics are no loving words
to arouse the females' passion
but addressed to other, smaller birds
clothed in blue and yellow fashion.

'Hey, you snivelling little tit!'
This blackbird's really saying,
'It's not your tree; get out of it!'
Which is awfully dismaying.

Graham Bruce Fletcher

Warm Day During the Covid-19 Lockdown

Audio

Suddenly, pond becomes snake,
sun-glassy sheets buckling.
Six layers move in coils, in loops,
laminate skin swelling and contracting,
olive green, dead-leaf brown,
a zoetrope of markings
discovering the frictive nature of water,
the slabs and scarps of waterlily,
the porridge of pondweed parts.

A blue clearing in the vegetation
reflects clumps of trees.
Our fat toad is stricken,
site fidelity, the smell of water molecules
the scoop of leaf
compacted in his membranes.

The head unhinges,
yellow collar rears, bucks above the water,
the tail is liquid,
toad fuelled,
helix volutions.

Now I fear for birds that
drink at the pond's edge,
and other small things at risk of harm.

Sophie Livingston

Some Haiku

1.
To find an answer
ask only perfect questions.
Those which no one knows.

2.
On the empty streets
the badger prowls in safety.
Nature fighting back.

3.
Below a mountain
the old river plots revenge
and wins its freedom.

4.
Decision makers,
embroiled in viral madness.
No one knows the truth.

5.
Undeterred by trees,
oblivious to all things,
the breeze slithers by.

Dave Walklett

First published in 2021−Still Together 2020.

Within the Calm

We'll rage as we fall from the wrangling arms of our gods,
messing the earth with our flesh,
fighting the gravity we feared in spring
when we hid their nudity in green.

In the still we wait.

We'll rage in grief and fall united
leaf by leaf we'll bare their veins,
their greedy branches will claw at empty skies
and ice cut in,
disease take hold,
and winter's force will tear their limbs.

Biography

Tina Baker

Why I write

'For me, to not write is to not dream. Writing is a way of freeing the mind of a million stories which are constantly being created and stored. The satisfaction of producing something good, something that creates a reaction, an emotion, outweighs the effort of clearing out the attic now and then.'

River

Audio

rived dipped foot from shin.

Braided rush of fall water, flinging
mountain gorges at a delicate reed,
submerging knees then belly.

Armoury of the clouds, forged
in glacial valleys, sculpting
taut skin.

Ankle drags, slow motion,
as current sweeps,
       false footing.

Skirting her fear, she lowers,
body merges,
   rollicking gush grips
her neck, fills ears, assaults
     her eyes.

Debris tumbles
     her thighs, compact mass
         of muscle sputtering.
Arms thrust through, bright
    blood and cold breath, heart beating hot.

Straightening,
    air brushes her,
        setting skin alight.

Clare Roberts

Destination

Audio

Veins stand proud on the peaks,
gouged with scars coursing
water's path to the deep,
       crossing the shoreline.

Heat flares from his nostrils as thickset arms heave,
oars slicing black butter.
Raindrops shoot the surface like bullets,
battalions stalking the breeze.

Then a gust –
       pressing fresh droplets full-face
like a non-stopping train steals from lungs, in a tunnel.

Shifting shadows slink, moon gleam
shifting perspectives as mountain tops glower.

His hood flicks his vision as the boat skitters
sideways, lurching, groaning for a mooring.
Flashlight flames, making mercury.

He glimpses skeleton frost reaching
into dark waters, the stones of a jetty –
a hovel glowing orange.

Clare Roberts

Legacy

Rosemary, dear, I can only hope you get this, when – and if – things return to normal. It's been quite unbearable; not being able to get in contact to make sure you're all safe and well. To be honest, absolutely everything here's been... a bit difficult...

I'm afraid Daddy's dead, dear. It looks rather as if I might be too, by the time you hear this recording, but it can't be helped. So, whatever happens, be sure to keep your chin up and look after the children. Who'd have thought we'd lose touch like this? When we heard the fires in Australia could mean you'd lose your power station, we realised we mightn't be able to Skype for a while, but we did think that by Christmas everything would be settled again, and the children could see their Granny and Grandpa and show us their presents. What a disappointment. I do hope you haven't had an utterly ghastly time.

We joked then – do you remember – that you ought to have all the water from our floods and we'd gladly swop it for some of your heatwave temperatures to dry everything out. Now all our water is frozen solid. I won't mention our sewage.

I wonder if you all knew when our winter set in. When, suddenly and unexpectedly, everywhere across Europe and North America came to a halt. At first it seemed we'd enjoy a white Christmas. Crosby's song: 'Just like the ones we used to know.'

Out here in the sticks we're quite inured to the occasional power cut, so Daddy just started up the generator. When the Radio, TV, 'phone and Broadband all stopped too, we reasoned it was perhaps power failing further afield. We saw the electricity cables come down just over the valley. The ice had got so thick, Daddy said, the pylons couldn't take the weight. When the generator ran out of diesel the drifts were so deep, we couldn't get to it anyway to try to refill the tank. One awful thing after another. Quite atrocious.

We slept a lot. It always seemed too dark to do much else. You'll be glad to hear; we didn't get fat. Not enough food – we had to ration it. Plenty of exercise chopping up stuff to feed the log-burner.

Daddy shot one of a pack of stray dogs. It lasted us through a week or so. To be frightfully honest, I thought it would taste horrid, but I can admit it was nicer than the Fortnum's tinned turkey we had at Christmas. It's surprising what you discover when you have to. Needs must! Thankful for small mercies.

At first it was all quite beautiful. That enchanting silence, the clean, pure-white scene. The World setting a fresh white linen tablecloth for spring to lay out the Hors d'Oeuvres of the riches summer promised to provide for our autumn harvest. It's all palled somewhat, but I do try to stay positive.

If Daddy hadn't been killed, I'd have run out of food already, but it won't be long now – unless something happens to relieve this continual grey winter. I've tried to keep track, I've wound the long-case clock, even though I've had to feed most of its woodwork to the log-burner, along with the antique furniture and floorboards – except for what's left in the warm-space we made back in January around the stove.

I think today's April 23rd. Saint George's Day. Shakespeare's birthday. I've been marking the calendar you and the children sent us from Australia for Christmas. Something to celebrate. Possibly.

'O, to be in England now that April's there.' I don't think Browning would say that now. I wonder how things are abroad. Is there anywhere else..? Is there somewhere left where people are still able to live as God intended? I suppose where there's life there's hope.

Whenever I start to think the only Browning I could put to good use would be the pistol, rather than the poet, I remind myself I owe it to you and the children – and to Daddy – not to give up. Nonetheless it does seem a dreadful pity, you know.

Daddy was determined to protect me. When a nasty, common boy tried to break into the house in February. He said he had to do it. The boy was clearly a ne'er-do-well. He was wearing one of those rebarbative baseball caps with the peak pointing backwards.

You know the type. After he'd shot him, Daddy went back to make sure he wouldn't get up again. They seem to have such vigour, the criminal types. I saw the boy seize Daddy's coat then slash and stab him to death. The blood steamed as it soaked into the snow, I didn't realise people are warm enough for that to happen. When everything thaws, they'll find them together. I expect they'll be like those ice mummies found in the glaciers when they began to melt.

I wonder if it will come soon enough for me to see it. Who knows? I mean; they never predicted climate change would bring about four months of endless winter. That it would be sudden, and not gradual. Like when there's an avalanche of snow off a roof when the sun shines. Not that the sun does shine. Perpetual grey. Ceaseless blizzards. Not what we expect of springtime.

To think; before all this, we worried about Trump starting a nuclear war, or Brexit destroying the economy. Do you think there might be some kind of poetic justice in all of this? I mean; we spoiled the weather, and now it's killed so many of us. Even an ark wouldn't help. I'm sure Daddy and I were among the least to blame.

If you do ever get this, I'm not sure there'll be anything left of any value for you and the children. My jewellery, and the family silver of course. I've chopped up and burned rather a lot of the house woodwork and furniture, sorry!

On the positive side, I've given up smoking. No Dunhills for months, now. Kept my lighter for the log-burner.

I'm down to the last few tins. And some jars. Strange things from the corners of the pantry. Palm hearts. Salsify. Anchovies. Pickled Walnuts. I'll have to melt quite a bit of ice in the pan on the log-burner to get enough water to counter the salty anchovies. I do miss tea. I think that's been the most inconvenient aspect. Never mind.

Ho-hum! Chin-up, dear.

Love to you all, John, and the children, dear, signing off now. Bye to you all from ...Mummy.

Graham Bruce Fletcher

3. LOVE

'WHERE THERE IS LOVE THERE IS LIFE.'

MAHATMA GANDHI

A Better View

Audio

over here? he says
unshouldering his rucksack
as wind wishes around them.

Droplets patter,
breath rushes ahead
as chest taps time,
memory alert under rustling
hood, ears snug against chilly mizzle.

She adjusts, balances, boots
glissading,
embraces his gaze, strong
hands steadying, securing.

His voice conjures city breaks,
an Alpine range, Edinburgh lights,
a gallery of Venetian glories.

Here, now, Leckhampton drenched
with Lakeland rain,
the panorama beyond
their gaze, telescoped
into a single moment
          of asking.

Rain burns her cheeks, distant
houses and roads hovering.

Fizz of thoughts tickles lips.

They had walked full circle,
conversation gleaming promise
with the clarity of a diamond.

She grew roots, swaying gently,
head in the mist
        and said yes.

Clare Roberts

Biography

Why I write

'I like to play with words as if they were coloured gems. Poetry can capture or release feelings, defy demons, enhance an experience of beauty or encapsulate a moment. Writing helps me realise inner visions, create an album of my past, and connect with others. Exercising creativity can feel powerful, transformational and cathartic, which sharpens my awareness of the world.'

Bee or Not Bee

Audio

I live to pollenate, fertilise
the fragrant moment;
hung on air in dusty dryness;
carried fleetingly like smoke in stillness.

This incense carpets my senses
as buzzing urgency
dances out my quest:
not scent, nor colour, only sun.

Taking sweetness
giving fruitfulness
my driven purpose;
to share; disclose.

This will; not my own
my brothers too follow
my dance
as I theirs.

My Queen is many:
in each incarnation her hunger
feeds me
my brothers, my children.

The fertile seed continues
my sons shall seek the flower
driven by the same dance
to satisfy their Queen.

All life is fuel to burn
all memories are ash
hung on the heat of the moment,
fallen onto the sheet.

Past desire
shall burn no more.
The pregnant pause
drained in fullness.

Dirty with dreams,
I fly
as the wind
breathes.

This winter, my empty husk shall blow away.

Graham Bruce Fletcher

Louis the Painter

Louis had not always been a painter. He had once been a barrister. It was said that Louis could take a tale and bend it, so it had no end and no beginning and that when he had finished with it, even the guiltiest of men would mistrust his memory and believe himself innocent.

He was a dark, tall man with bones as awkward as a deck chair and a stinging manner. Talking to him was like walking through a nettle patch, and a person couldn't say 'good day' without carrying a transcript of the most recent meteorological report to hand over for his scrutiny. In his thirties, he had inherited a grand house on a marsh-filled island off the coast of Kent, which he filled with books and paintings. Though he was civil to his neighbours, he was not inclined to invite them into his home, for he felt most comfortable talking to someone across a table in a police cell.

And so he lived until the age of forty when, without warning, he married, leaving the whole island wondering and shocked.

Agata was Norwegian and a musician. They had met in London at a reception that followed one of her concerts. She was a violinist but did not play the kinds of jigs you can dance to after a few drinks. Hers was strange, thin music that spoke of ice and death, and at first, it was this music that people put the marriage down to. Louis being so strange and icy himself, they said, perhaps she had been homesick and found in him the quiet, sad spaces she missed. She was also beautiful but came from a country where beauty is as common as pebbles. She did not regard her looks, except occasionally, when she saw them reflected in other people's startled glances. In the face of her beauty and Louis's lack of it, Joe Spade claimed she had been accused of murder and that marriage was the price Louis had demanded for getting her off, but no one believed him for more than a day or two.

A week after his wedding, Louis announced a party to celebrate his marriage. Invitations were sent to a hundred people, but three hundred turned up, spilling on a warm night out into the gardens and down the steps onto the beach. The uninvited guests brought their own drinks and chairs out of politeness and pumped Louis' hand up and down in congratulations wanting a share of his miracle, for Louis was transformed. He smiled, and his smile was like the stagger of a new-born lamb. At last, Louis' bones had found their slot. He now stood tall and straight, one arm around his wife's waist, the other clasping hands or waving for more beer and champagne.

Those that had never liked him remembered now that his father had been a hard, cruel man and had not loved his son and that his mother had drowned herself when he was seven – so that Louis' childhood had been a queer lonely thing – and drank another glass to his health. And those that he had defended forgave him their shame; remembered only that he had shaken their hand, man to man, after the verdict, and they vowed to steal only worthless items from the party, as keepsakes.

'My wife and I,' Louis kept saying. 'My wife and I,' and his wife looked at him, and the guests could see that, even if she was a murderer, she had married him for love and not freedom and shook his hand a little more in the hope that his miracle would rub off a little on themselves.

And so it continued for a year. Louis and his wife would spend weeks in London and weeks on the island. Louis' wife would talk to the fisherman about Norway in her strange accent, and on windless nights the sound of her cold music could be heard in the village, and Louis, sitting by the fire, would put down his book to watch his wife play. And so, it might have continued if Louis had not had a secret.

It sometimes happens that when a man has more happiness than he thinks he deserves, he cannot stop fearing that he will be found out and that happiness will abandon him. And so it was with Louis. He knew he did not deserve his wife. However hard he argued his case with himself; however skillfully he highlighted his virtues and downplayed his vices, however carefully he bent his story so that it had no beginning and no end, his verdict was always the same. He was guilty of stealing his wife from someone better than himself.

And this idea began to prey on Louis and keep him awake at night. He would quietly tuck the duvet round her shoulders, creep downstairs and sit shivering and worrying. 'What is wrong?' she would ask him, some evenings, putting down her violin and coming to kneel alongside him by the chair. But he told her that nothing was wrong and so she knew he had a secret that he was keeping from her.

In desperation, he began to paint, seeking in himself that ability to express rather than argue that he so admired in her. If I can create just one beautiful thing, he thought, it would prove that I am not entirely worthless.

His paintings were no good. He worked harder. He bought a little studio up a flight of seven steps, thinking the light and the privacy might help. It didn't. He grew more desperate and neglected the law for lessons in London and Paris. The paintings became a little better, but his legal practice dwindled. No one likes to think their crimes are uninteresting – particularly to their lawyers – and Louis was no longer interested.

When his wife came to tell him she was expecting a baby, he decided he might do better with portraits on large canvases and hammered six-foot by four-foot frames as she tried to rehearse. At this time, the storm stole the cliff from under his dark, grand house, leaving it uninhabitable and valueless. 'Surely, she will leave me now?' thought Louis, for he had come to hope his wife had married him for his money, that being the one thing he could offer her. She did not leave. Instead, their daughter was born in the small cottage alongside the studio where his unsold paintings filled one whole room.

He painted mother and baby in oils and then wept at his failure. He grew jealous of Agata's talent and the baby; sought to cut her down to his size.

'You're not so effing great yourself,' he would say when she asked him not to drink while the baby was awake.

There were other women.

'I am preparing,' he would sob to himself afterwards.

'I am preparing myself for when she leaves me.'

The day she left was a Wednesday. She did not tell him she was going but left a note pinned to the studio door. She took just one suitcase, her violin and their seven-year-old daughter and caught the 11.45 train stopping at Sittingbourne and Rochester.

People on the island said that Louis' heart shrivelled to the exact size and shape of a cobnut and that there was no room in it left for any kindly feeling anymore.

Sophie Livingston

Geography of a Love Affair

Audio

1. Welsh Mountain Tops

We sat there silent, breathless,
hearing the wind
and each other's thoughts,
watching the clouds
and each other's drift,
touching the rock
and each other's core.

2. Scottish Interlude

I remember that island in the loch,
across grey, wind-worried water.
The sun sulked
and birds flocked in disarray
behind the flimsy boat.
I couldn't tell you then;
perhaps I did not know myself.

3. Shropshire Sunday

The path rough with regrets,
we walk the Blue Remembered Hills
mindful of our step,
a widening fault between us.

Wind steals careful words
from faithless lips,
rounding the rocky outcrops
of our lives,
reflecting in dark pools
on blackened soil

until, in silence save for skylarks,
an end is reached
where heather hugs the hillside,
where Stone Age man
buried his dead.

Gill Garrett

First published in Waymarks, Graffiti Books 2020.

Tears

That first time I thought he was crying over spilt milk. He was in the kitchen; his bare feet surrounded by shards of glass, blood spreading a delta across the white pool.

'Poor glass!' He sobbed.

I'd never seen him cry before. Not painful injury, nor his mother's death. Not our burglary, nor when the cat was run over. Ever the strong and silent type.

He's out on the drive now, soothing the wheelie bin. He says the wind pushed it over and hurt it. His empathy for inanimate objects is growing stronger.

And he won't let me comfort him.

Graham Bruce Fletcher

This type of story, being exactly 100 words, not including the title, is known as a 'Drabble'.

Cook

Audio

Alone in the kitchen,
thoughts minced,
rage bubbling in pans as I chop,
slice out the sound of Mortal Combat.

Turn to iTunes -
reduce the heat. Schumann
calms to a simmer.

Teenage
son stomps, knives
out for the music.
Bickering blisters.

Door chits -
it's his stepfather, my love
muted in this moment.

He breezes in, dispelling
doubtful air.
Kitchen calms.

How do you do that?
Smiles spread
like butter and jam.

Clare Roberts

Familiarity

Audio

This familiarity of shape
breeds no contempt.
This movement of your body;
the division of hair at your nape
and precisely this flare to your shoulder
inviting the traverse of a necklace of kisses.

Rather, then, love has charted your landscape;
every contour known by my hand,
its remembered textures linger under my skin.
Your body my road home: my lips trace the path.
my mouth, in the garden, drinks
the aromatic well of your wishes.

This homecoming completes me:
the way these hairs curl; this hollow;
the inside of your thigh;
the weight of your breast;
the geography of your bones;
the constellations of your moles.

All I know of you reveals none of your mystery
for all my navigation.
Your homeliness: the imperfections you prefer to hide
I love the most.
Your hands: sausage fingers you wish were elegant.
Your feet concealed beneath the sheet.
The gentle fecundity of your belly.

When you're unashamed of these,
as you are of those parts you offer,
bidding me welcome,
bring yourself home complete,
to my familiar shape.

Graham Bruce Fletcher

Biography

Why I write

'My uncle was a writer. My father was
a Chartered Accountant. Words beat
numbers. No Contest when seeking a
role model. I love swopping stories
with folks. When I can't bend their ear,
I write it down. Life (being alive) is
interesting. I spy on it and try to show
it to people, so they can find what
they could see, if only they'd look.'

Origin of Species

Audio

*'The intervals between two horizontal
lines may represent a thousand
generations'*
Charles Darwin

Take this ant, he said,
At what point might he love?
(As far as the extreme intricacy of the subject permits.)
And pygmy three-toed sloth?
Tree rat? Giant sengi? Stubfoot toad?
The northern hairy wombat?
Take the mollusc; does he love?
Or is he subject to some irretrievable and secret switch,
Devoid of meaning: statistical in origin.
Arguably,
Pure?

We draw in the wildernesses, she replied,
differ, bleed,
swim in the many curious incidents
of ourselves.
I guess you slept with her, she said.

There is extinction.
The tiny share we have of time.
And there is love.

Sophie Livingston

First published in ARTEMISpoetry 2021.

Breathing Out

'We concentrate on the exhalation,' she said. He lay on the floor with the others and breathed out. 'How long can you hold that out breath before you inhale again?' she asked.

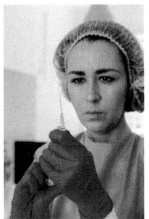

His bedroom had reminded him of student days – a single bed, a small ensuite and a pinboard for mementos. It had been murky when he'd left home – the sun a smear behind sour, yellowish clouds. He couldn't tell what the weather was now.

He joined a tour of the facilities – the swimming pool and sauna, yoga and Tai Chi classes. The evening meal was excellent. 'Can I go for a walk?' he asked. 'This is a sealed unit,' she replied, 'but we have virtual spring and autumn walks programmed in our leisure suites. Some guests prefer to jump straight to the views from mountain tops or from ships sailing west.' Her uniform was both crisp and concealing. It reminded him of nuns. 'How long?' he asked. 'Approximately a month,' she replied. 'We don't want to rush anyone. You are lucky,' she added, 'the state-run units are nothing like this.'

The place he loved and returned to again and again over the coming weeks was the poetry room. The poems, thousands of them, were written on A4 paper and protected from decay by sheets of glass fixed to the floors, walls and ceilings. 'It's beautiful,' he had exclaimed on first seeing it. She smiled and nodded. 'It seems to be an impulse,' she said, 'and we cherish them.'

His daughter had cried. His retirement notice arrived the day after his 70th birthday. He possessed savings enough to postpone it by five years but wanted his death to be his gift to her and his granddaughter. It was an act of love. 'The old must make way for the young,' he said as he kissed her goodbye. 'That is the way of things. I am happy.'

He read many of the poems. Often, they were awkward, shoddy things and this moved him more. What impulse was it that had led them to try and press some final expression of themselves into words they had rarely used in their lives? Was there some secret thing, revealed, at this moment of crisis in their existence, that demanded to be heard in this way?

'They are the tuneless songs of the dying,' he told her after he had, at last, asked for his own paper and pen. 'They are a final, blessed exhalation of something we cannot understand.'

'Close your eyes and breathe out gently,' she said.

Sophie Livingston

Biography

Why I write

'Writing is an exercise in power. To take someone on the journey I have imagined appeals to the control freak in me.'

Remember My Name

Where the hell is she?

Derek scans the shop fronts, irritated and weary. How could she be so invisible? The mall will be closing soon. There are only a few customers left, scurrying away from the bland piano music oozing from the PA system.

Derek breathes the plastic scented air and wishes he were back on the coach with his Wilbur Smith.

Is that her?

A flash of green at the back of a shop, so Derek walks inside, glad to have a purpose, glad to be away from the glare of the fluorescent lights. Jazzy saxophone music now; different, but equally bland.

The shop is filled with expensive, useless tat. Fancy Goods, they called it, in Derek's young day. Bowls of carved wooden fruit. Embroidered knee pads for gardeners. Draft excluders decorated as snakes.

A sullen teenager stands by the till and ignores him, mobile phone jammed between her shoulder and her ear. Her hands hover over the keys, awaiting some divine command.

At the back of the shop it's not Sheila's pashmina at all, but a young couple Derek doesn't recognise, in bright green fleeces. Derek turns away, fuming. And stops. He can't face the mall again; there's nowhere to sit, and his feet hurt. He turns back to the couple in green. Maybe he can start a conversation, pass the time of day.

The man is balding and round faced. Not what you would call handsome, but cheerful looking. The woman is attractive, in an untidy way. Big wide eyes, she has, and dark honey hair gathered loosely at the back of her head.

Derek moves closer, suddenly curious. This part of the shop is filled with souvenirs of Cerne Abbas, where the coach had stopped earlier. Tea towels, biscuit tins, cards, mugs; all showing the infamous chalk giant with its mighty, erect penis.

The couple in green snigger together, like children.

Derek lurks behind a small tree, decorated with red porcelain fruits. He breathes through his mouth, the better to hear what they're saying, his tongue tasting the air.

The man is holding something, showing it to the woman, both of them gasping with stifled laughter. The woman rests a hand on the man's shoulder, tilts her head back, closes those wide eyes, shakes with uncontrollable laughter.

Derek sees that it's a clock, the man is holding a clock, a simple metal circle of olive green, on which is painted the Cerne Abbas Giant. Its penis is the hour hand, slowly sweeping out the time. They laugh together, the couple in green, quietly, yet uncontrollably, completely oblivious to everything around them, as though they were the only two people left in the world.

Then she stops laughing. She leans over to the man and says something, quietly, her eyes wide as she gently, tenderly rests a finger on the giant's penis.

Back in the mall, shops are lowering their shutters and switching off their lights.

Derek marches through the cloying music, bewildered and angry. He imagines being locked inside the mall for the night, bedding down in the gents, keeping still for fear of setting off the alarms.

What did she say to him? What did she say that made him stop laughing?

Derek wonders what she's wearing, under her fleece. One of those T-shirts, maybe, like he sees on young people in the street; bizarre, obscene slogans, stuff he only half understands.

Remember my name: you'll be screaming it later.

Derek imagines them together, the couple in green, getting down to business in some motel, like in the videos Derek borrows from Norman next door. The beat, beat of the headboard against the wall, the wet slap of flesh on flesh, the moans, the crying out.

Derek thinks of that video he and Sheila once watched. Norman's wife brought it round, a romantic comedy they'd never got round to seeing at the cinema.

At one point, the leading couple had started making love; all wailing saxophones, passionate kissing, clothes being shed. Quite tame compared to Norman's videos, of course. Derek had wondered what Sheila would have said if it had jumped to the real thing, Norman cocking up maybe, getting his tapes mixed up.

As things were building to a climax, Sheila had tapped him on the knee, prodded him until he had turned to look at her, wild impossible thoughts forming in his head.

'Those are the floor tiles I was telling you about,' she had said, pointing to the screen. 'The ones in Mrs Menzies downstairs toilet.'

Derek thinks of his and Sheila's infrequent couplings. Midweek afternoons, the rain beating on the double glazing. What does she think, as he grunts away? What goes through her mind?

'Get a, Get a move on, will you? I'm missing *Countdown*.'

'What are you doing here, Derek?' Sheila rails at him, drops of saliva landing on his glasses. 'I told you to stay on the coach!' Her hands are filled with bright new carrier bags, her breath smells of coffee. She's not even wearing the pashmina.

'Thirty-five pounds for the clock,' says a frowning stranger, who is suddenly the bored teenager from the Cerne Abbas shop.

'Thirty-five and I'll not press charges.' A fat security man stands behind her, arms folded.

Derek looks down at his hands, his sweating red hands, holding the dark green clock with its chalk giant and its penis hour hand, and the tears run down his face, and he can't stop them, no matter how hard he tries.

Stephen Connolly   *Audio*

First published in The Quiet Feather 2006.

An Autistic Child

Audio

Fluent at six
you read as if by instinct,
concentrating for hours,
cocooned within your world
of words.

'A gifted child'
they said.

But to spread your wings,
to interact, you must read
between the lines,
decode the syntax of expression
interpret posture, gesture, space,
leaf through the pages
of the human face.

Not yours the gift that makes
for easy friendship, give and take,
acceptance by the crowd.
Such literacy a mystery to you –
a lesson to be learned
piecemeal over years.

Easier by far
the comfort of your books.

Gill Garrett
Winning entry Onward Poetry Competition 2013.

4. INDUSTRY

'SLOTH MAKES ALL THINGS DIFFICULT
BUT INDUSTRY ALL THINGS EASY.'

BENJAMIN FRANKLIN

Playing Chess in a Steelworks

Audio

Evening masks the soot on weathered
walls. They shudder as somewhere
a hammer booms, bashing metal
into pre-planned shapes and patterns.

The air is steam and sulphur. Sequestered
in the works canteen from cranes and hoists
and tubes of unfettled steel, we meet, steel-men
and council staff, drawn to the sixty-four squares

and a very civil war of knights and rooks.
Outside there's no room for mistakes.
Here, infinite scope to be lost
in strategies and branching variations,

silent save for a sip of tea and biscuit crunch,
face-to-face, intent on conquest.
Act and react, play on the edge and later,
conduct a post-mortem where no one really died.

Drive home. The sky is furnace-lit.

Frank McMahon

The Tin Miners

Camborne, Cornwall, 1801

James would often drink in the pub and listen to the tales his workmates would tell. They were older miners, his father Henry included, who worked and drank hard. Ribald stories were told of their lives before the mine, working the land from sun-beamed dawn to midge-ridden dusk.

They would speak longingly of the sensory delights of the countryside from the blackberry to the columbine and would embroider tales of assignations amongst the meadows with young maids of a willing and eager nature.

As peasant farm labourers, they had been poor, and their lives were at the mercy of the elements. There were cold winters, late springs, drought, flood, and famine, but in retrospect, living on the land seemed infinitely better than crouching far from the light of day, in a cold and wet miner's stall.

All the men who would assemble in the pub were comparatively short in stature but had broad shoulders, muscular arms and strong backs. These were men who broke 'hard rock' in search of copper and tin deposits. The rock they mined was granite, not softer sandstone or brittle slate. To get to the mine face, the men would climb rope ladders to varying depths, where 'roads' ran for half a mile before the working face was reached. The miners would dig at the rock that lay beneath the Atlantic Ocean.

The conditions in the mine were appalling. The minimal light was from candles, mounted on the leather helmets worn by the miners. The walls and floors of the tunnels were running wet from groundwater, and the heat at such depths meant men worked in boots and trousers;

their upper bodies, left bare, would accumulate scars from injuries sustained throughout their working life. The ore-bearing seams would be narrow, so mining was carried out in cramped and miserable conditions. There wasn't the room for big men at the workface. Brute force was needed to excavate the required daily tonnage, using steel picks, mandrills, sledgehammers and shovels. Cooperation between the miners was essential, as lives depended on it.

The use of the mandrill and sledgehammer was the most dangerous operation. Two men worked within each narrow stall. One would hold the inch diameter mandrill, ensuring the shaft was square with the workface, whilst the other would strike at its end with the sledge, driving the hardened steel tip into the rock. To be holding the mandrill was to be at the mercy of your workmate who administered the blows. Trust between the two men was essential. The mandrill had to be held with a steady and firm grip, and the sledge was to be swung accurately and precisely, blow after blow in rhythmic succession. Accidents happened, and an injury to hands, arms, shoulders and, worst of all, the head, was common.

The hewn rock containing the ore would be shovelled away from the workface and then dragged in wagons by hauliers to the lift shaft. Hauliers were often children. If they survived into adulthood, they would replace the miners at the face who were lost by attrition to accident or ill-health. The youths served their grim apprenticeship in the pitch-black tunnels and galleries of the mine, gaining strength and experience as each terror was overcome.

Every tragic death of a miner, haulier or labourer would be rationalised as a reprieve for those who remained. The longer a miner lived, the more he was able to cope, and his chances of surviving the next day would be that bit better. It had been that way for all the men in the pub this Christmas Eve. They had survived into adulthood and avoided being taken by the chance event of a fall of rock, a careering wagon or the blow of a carelessly wielded hammer.

Silicosis was a major killer for the veteran hard-rock miner; rock dust choked the throat and invaded the lungs. For those with 'the dust', it often seemed like no amount of coughing would loosen the grit accumulated in their chest. The phlegm produced by the body gave some relief, once coughed up and spat out, but if you were in the grip of the dust, your days were numbered. Its effects were cumulative, and as Henry was forty-six, his days and nights were racked with bouts of coughing fits. His breath would wheeze from his throat and his speech would be punctuated by gasps for air. For Henry, the final nightmare had begun.

Mining was their life, and for almost all of them, it would be their death.

Audio

Selwyn Morgan

James, and his father, Henry, were tin miners in Camborne, Cornwall, 1801. Richard Trevithick was their Mining Engineer. This passage is taken from the novel, Going Up Camborne Hill, Amazon 2020.

Biography

Why I write

'I love the process... Being amongst words and bringing to life my ideas by way of the sentence arrangement and punctuation; ensuring, as best I can, the subtleties and nuances of the language gives room for the reader to understand my intention.'

Vermeer

Audio

In another plague year
The shops and schools are closed
A baby in the next room is crying again,
But Vermeer is mixing pigments
And cannot help.
Vermillion, azurite and indigo with silica grind.
Looking out again to the street below
He is waiting for the boy.

Sweat soaks his shirt
His long hair reeking of oil and turpentine
Slowly, slowly the paint goes on
Horizontal and vertical frames
He is waiting for the boy.

Like him in a second-floor room
In a house in Delft
The 'Girl Reading a Letter''
Is close to a window
In a cool morning light.
Both are waiting, waiting for the boy

At last the tousled head is at the door.
'Let him in' he cries
To his many children down below
And Catherina labouring at the stove.
Never mind the crippling debts
Now he has his lapis lazuli, his ultramarine
Now he can paint the chair.

Clare Finnimore

The Compositor

I heard it fall. I was sleeping but I heard it fall. The dull thud of it landing on the mat had woken me. What was I dreaming? Yes, I remember, I had been dreaming of running away from this drain of a town.

The envelope is the colour of business, cold tea in a chipped mug, a shade of brown neither here nor there. My name and address have been hand written, the ink evenly distributed from the nib. In school I struggled with writing. In my eagerness my hand always made the nib splay. I kept a square of blotting paper close by drenched black and blue with the evidence of my mistakes. Whoever sealed this envelope knew the news before me. I've spent most of my life knowing that.

I tighten the strings of my pyjama bottoms then pick up the envelope and take it into the kitchen. I light a cigarette and watch as the smoke curls around my face. The taste of whisky rises in my throat, and that reckless thirst. Through the fug of smoke in the dark panelled room of a pub in London's Fleet Street, my colleagues and friends drink, drink to sate the thirst created by the hot, dirty chaotic world of the composition room; a factory crammed with word machines, editors, sub editors, journalists, and compositors. They are hungry, too, for a story, the next deadline, but now they drink, laughing with their mouths wide open ready for the next round.

I put the envelope on the small kitchen table which I bought thirty years ago thinking it would make do until my world expanded; a wife, maybe a couple of children. More mess. I look around the kitchen for Shoo. At first he visited under the cover of night, leaving his glossy black droppings on the worktop, then he got brave, appearing in the day. A mutual cycle has evolved; I clear his droppings and he clears mine, mostly the crumbs of digestive biscuits or toasted bread. I should clear up after myself but I would miss him. A dog needs walking, I need energy to walk. I get confused. I can't be trusted. Panic rising! I check the clock. The sound of metal rains down, the frantic clatter of keys, the roar of monstrous typewriters, warning bells for mistakes, warning bells for justification, throw in those ingots, top up that pot, and all the while the room hotting with the fumes of molten lead. The thirst is building. I check the clock again. I need time. Give me slugs, give me a plate, give me this day my daily words! Words to make an even line, to fill a row, to make a page. Faster faster and make no mistakes, space and time is running out.

I should open the envelope even though I know what's inside. Any curiosity is redundant now. It's the end of an era. Time to move on, time to change. I don't need to read the final result from forty years of composing. I just want to remember the community I've lost not the fallout, remember all the good people, my friends.

She was pretty, a sub editor. Across the stone she watched my dexterous black-inked fingers shuffle slugs of lead. She wasn't permitted to handle the text so together we talked the news into place, discovering ways for me to compress the facts and the lies, the good news and the bad, to somehow make it all fit, and always keeping the stone between us. That was the rule. That's how it was back then.

My fingers are black and my skin is yellow but I still long for that reckless hunger, that insatiable thirst, that clock. It's a different time now. Things have moved on but deadlines remain, thank God.

Shoo breaks cover. He knows I'm here and will tolerate me if I don't move so I freeze. Such power he has, or is it a spell? Would he freeze for me? Would he wait and watch as I removed his waste?

Crabbe's poem, 'The Newspaper', runs in my head...

'In what rare production shall we trace
Such various subjects in so small a space?'

I compose myself. There will be no going back, no room for error. I take a breath before plunging my hands into my stomach. I feel around until I find it. My liver comes away easily. I look at it, limp in my hands, grey and fatty... I check the clock.

Here it comes, another launch, another deadline, ***Audio*** and all begins again.

Tina Baker

56

5. FUN AND GAMES

'BE HAPPY FOR THIS MOMENT.
THIS MOMENT IS YOUR LIFE.'

OMAR KHAYYAM

Things to Do Everyday

Audio

Every day I shall paint a picture
Composition, contrast, colour, impact

Every day I shall read a poem
For love of sounds
Hidden meanings, lasting thoughts

Every day I shall dance
Pounding my feet, whirling, leaping
Stretching my muscles
Lifting my soul

Every day I shall sing a song
Practise scales and arpeggios
For sheer joy
Knowing I will annoy my neighbours
And my cats will try to comfort me

Every day I shall walk in the garden
Talk to flowers
Plant something new
Move weeds to better places
Train over-enthusiastic climbers
Where they suffocate slow shy shoots

Every day I will write
A story, poem, play
With words, people, places, plots, secrets.
They wait inside my head
Like an angel in stone
For this sculptor to find them.

Bridget Arregger

The Five-Cent Slots

Audio

Five cents a go was all it took,
to play the game but not get hooked.
To watch high rollers play fast and free,
without a thought about their n^{th} degree,
when winnings fell below their loss
(and believing they gave not a toss),
they blew their luck away.

The black bunny came, with bobtail white,
and offered drinks throughout the night;
'Upon the house', she would announce,
and I'd play the game; for a dollar's flounce
would bring her back with my request;
'The casino's favourite, I behest':
(a margarita on a silver tray).

Sometimes I'd win, sometimes I'd lose,
and five cents a go did not abuse
my wallet, nor my sense of worth;
and kept my expectations down to earth.
But as my five-cent pot got slimmer,
and my hopes of wealth got dimmer,
another margarita was on its way.

Selwyn Morgan

Why I Don't
Go Jogging Anymore

Audio

There was an old jogger called Hatherly
Who went out each morning and Saturday
She ran up and down
And all round the town
With her bosoms going flapperty, flapperty.

Bridget Arregger

A Spree

Audio

Manikins behind shop windows, spring
in our step,
the day fashioned for our fun.

Arms draped with possibility, we try on our future selves,
take the change,
and turn, skitting along the pavement.

Bags jostle thighs, happy hours
ahead, as we sidestep
the crowds, waltz
the winding streets.

Pit-stop flutes
bubble up remembered stories.

Coins chink and notes rustle.
Fabric stacks slide
neatly in paper packages.

We step lightly
into our tomorrows.

Clare Roberts

Dear Samuel Johnson,

I've been taking your advice,
but all the cheques in the post
turn out to be rejection slips.

Samuel Johnson once said; 'Write only for money.'
But the market these days is for verse that's dead funny
The serious matter, not made to amuse
Just isn't popular; publishers refuse.

I've been writing these poems, but I've got trouble with 'em;
I just can't get rid of the rhyme and the rhythm.
Whatever I do, I am sorry to say,
This sense of tradition just won't go away.

Professional poets can soon spot an amateur –
They're the ones who write rhymes in iambic-pentameter.
I fill mine with clichés, their meaning's so dense,
They sound all sententious and filled with fresh sense.

You see, I think Life is a Great Cosmic Joke
And I want to write poems to tell it to folk.
I'd like to talk straight, in a voice that's vernacular,
And write down the Truth in a style that's spectacular.

But I scribble around, with my head up my arse,
And turn out this stuff that's pronounced 'Middle-Class'
I end up conforming just like an old Laureate
So critics and publishers simply ignore it.

I'm out of control; my career's on the skids
So I've got to do something for my wife and four kids.
No-one will employ me, because poets are weird
Even though I've cut off all my hair and my beard.

Maybe some light stuff could start me on a roll,
And writing could help me to sign off the dole.
I might not be a rapper, but I've still got to write
And I'm sorry this poem's turned out to be ....

Graham Bruce Fletcher

Dennis Kelly

Audio

Dennis Kelly loved his telly;
watched it all the time.
Dad said: 'Son,
your eyes'll go square,
your brain'll turn to slime.'

But Dennis Kelly kept watching telly:
laughed at what his dad said.
'til one day in the mirror it shocked him to see
there was *STUFF* coming out of his head.

It oozed from his nose, from his mouth and his ears;
out from his eye sockets too.
And ten minutes later all that was left
was a Dennis-sized pile of *GOO*.

Dad shouted loudly, 'I told you so!'
but his Mum just cried and cried.
They scooped the *GOO* into a pot
and set it beside their bedside.

And now to the moral of this sorry tale:
be careful what you do.
Don't watch too much telly
Like poor Dennis Kelly:
You might end up as GOO too.

Dave Walklett

Gudmundower's Soup

Gudmundower was frightened. He did not understand where, or why, he was there. And then someone approached.

'Where am I? What is this place and who are you?' he stammered nervously.

'I am St Peter, and you are at the Pearly Gates.'

St Peter could see that this meant nothing at all to the fearful peasant before him.

'Let me explain. This is a prelaunch trial and you, my friend, are one of the lucky ones! You see, this is Heaven, and it is where God lives!'

'Ogfrin the Almighty?' Gudmundower's eyes were wide open, and he backed away.

'No, no. I'm afraid Ogfrin does not exist. Nor do all those gods that other tribes worship. You see Gudmundower, there is only one god – God – and he did everything to create the world and all the creatures in it. Then He sat back, and before He knew it, there were a thousand other gods all getting the credit. So, this is our master plan. In a few years God will send His son to earth to prove to everyone that there is only one God.

'I never knew that?'

'Part of the deal is that when men die, they will arrive at these Pearly Gates, and I will review their lives and decide whether they should come in here – Heaven – for the rest of eternity or be damned and go to Hell. You're one of the lucky ones because we haven't finished building Hell yet. It was supposed to be up and running but Satan is way over his promised delivery date and the budget is all to blazes. The latest excuse is that the fiery furnaces keep melting.'

St Peter fished around in his robe, looking for the notes on Gudmundower's life whilst the peasant looked nervously around him. 'Ah! Here we are. Now I know I said you'd be coming in here anyway, but I need to practise my assessments, so please humour me for a little longer as I go through your files. Right, let's see.'

He paused as he read the notes on Gudmundower's life, making little noises as he read.

'OK, not too bad. I see you've done a fair bit of poaching, but we won't worry about that. God put all the animals and fishes and birds on earth for everyone... You have a wife, Frigor, and seven children.'

He read on, mumbling occasionally. Gudmundower could not believe that someone he had never met before knew so much. He wondered if this was a strange dream resulting from the magic soup.

'Ah, now,' St Peter interrupted his musings, 'overall that's not too bad. I don't think you'd have been going to Hell anyway, but my notes only go up to yesterday, so you'd better fill me in on what brought you here.'

'It was no crime, sire!' Gudmundower implored with all his expressive power.

'Tell me all.'

'You see, I'm a charcoal burner and I work in the forest. My little child Urgo was sick with the fever yesterday and Frigor said that I must bring home some of the special herbs to cure her. After I had finished, I went deep into the forest to search, and it was getting dark. I had to go into the Badlands before I could find any.'

'The Badlands...? That's not wise.'

'I missed my path and wandered into a glade where there were two old hags around a fire, and I was much affeared!'

His story was tumbling from his lips, like a flood of relief, and his eyes were distant as he searched his mind for the right words as he relived last night's events.

'Go on,' said St Peter, adding to his notes with a stubby pencil.

'The old crones had a very bad reputation and everyone in the village was frightened of that part of the woods, because they say the crones rule it with evil spirits... But, they saw me and called me over. They were very friendly. They invited me to join them for something to eat before returning home. They had a stew of mushrooms and herbs, and I was very hungry and frightened of what they might do if I spurned their hospitality... so I said 'yes'.

'Oh!' St Peter made a note.

'We sat while it cooked and I told them of the fears of the villagers, and they were much amused. There were various things hanging in the trees around us which they said were placed there to keep strangers away because they were afraid of being attacked.'

'So as to ward off evil intent?'

'I supposed so. When I looked up, I could see from the light from the fire a dead cat, a human skull and a noose. I shivered. Anyway, I had the soup, and it was very good, and we all became much happier. They insisted I have a second bowlful.'

'Who wouldn't? It sounds delicious.'

'I said that I, Gudmundower, was also a man of the forest and had worked with trees all my life and they were mistaken if they thought the noose would frighten people.'

'Oh? Why not?'

'The branch! It was too weak to take the weight. I even showed them...They were very grateful to me.' Gudmundower was reflective.

'I stood on a log and put the noose around my neck,' he spoke slowly as his grubby hand went up to the back of his neck where the knot had tightened, 'and I jumped off.... and now... I'm here?'

The words trailed away, and he stood frowning, trying to reconcile the trick his new friends had played on him. He looked up.

'The herbs. I still have the herbs.' His voice rose. 'Frigor will never forgive me! Please, I must go back. It is important – oh, please.'

'I'm sorry! That's not possible. But be reassured, the child will recover. I promise you. Now come along, it's time for you to come inside as there's someone else on their way.'

Richard Lutwyche

Richard's stories have been reproduced with the kind permission of Valerie Lutwyche.
Richard joined the group in 2015 and delighted us with his humorous short stories, often based on his farming experience and unbounded knowledge of rare breeds of British pigs. Richard, died in 2021. He is missed.

Gobsmacked

'How much did you say was that pushbike?' said Dad.

'Six pounds, seventeen and sixpence!'

'What...!' said Dad. 'Do you know how many ha'pennies that is?'

It was always a worry when my dad was about to express our proposed purchases in half-pennies, never mind farthings, and it was for three reasons:

One: there was no point arguing that he must be mistaken, because he never was.

Two: anything that was counted in 'ha'pennies' sounded too much to pay for... well... anything; apart from a gobstopper.

Three: the clincher... no matter how hard we tried, we were not going to get what we wanted.

He was a whiz at mental arithmetic, my dad. Of course, time and the fall of the British Empire caught up with him: we grew up and could afford to buy our own bike, and Great Britain succumbed to the 'foreign' notion of decimalisation. Forevermore, every Tom, Dick or Henrietta could tell you how many ha'pennies were in as many pounds as you might mention, simply by multiplying by two and adding two zeros.

His love of numbers, and the fun to be had from playing around with them, has been passed down to me, and it surfaces at odd times. Recently, in a bar in town, I ordered a half-pint of beer.

'That'll be two pounds and twenty pence, please.' said the barman, and I reached for my card to waft it, Harry Potter-like, at the payment machine... I hesitated...

I had a flash of memory. A memory of drinking a beer with my dad in the working men's club in our village; it would have been the mid-1960s.

No matter what people say about the real ales of the past, the stuff they served up in that club was rubbish; but it was cheap. On high days and holidays, it was reduced in price to one shilling and three pence a pint.

Returning to the reality of 2022 and the moist glass set before me, my mind went mental; arithmetically, that is. Bear with me.

In 1966, there were 20 shillings in one pound, and one shilling consisted of 12 pence. Now, if you divide one shilling and threepence (15 old pence) into one pound (240 old pence), it equals sixteen pints per pound... easy! It follows that two pounds would buy you 32 pints, and the twenty new pence (one-fifth of a pound, being 48 old pence), would have bought three-and-a-bit pints. That would make...

'Thirty-five,' I said out loud.

'No...! Two pounds, twenty,' came the reply.

'No...? What I meant was, when I was your age, I could buy thirty-five pints for what I've just given you for half a pint... and I could have left a tip... I admit, yours is better beer, but, even so, it makes you wonder.'

'Very interesting' he said, in a very disinterested way. 'Would you like a pint instead?'

'Not at these prices,' I laughed.

He failed to see the humour in it, but gave me time, with due respect to my age, to get over it. I waved my card at his machine to show that I, too, could be a member of the biometric, electronic, cash-free generation…

It made me think... *How times have changed...*

I felt a twinge of nostalgic bitter-sweetness. For I no longer carried in my pocket the weight of enough old change to pay two shillings and eleven pence for a curry on a Friday night... and, worse still, the gift of numbers passed on to me by my dad had become a waste of time… for one barman, at least.

Audio

Selwyn Morgan

First published in Cirencester Scene 2020, entitled How Much!.

The Awkward Shopper
(From the Tales of Temple Monkton series)

Some farmers scraped a living from a smallholding, but at the other end of the scale were real agronomists. One of the leaders, farming 1500 acres of prime arable land, was Johnny, who had inherited his country estate.

Although his voice could at times sound 'plummy', you'd never know from looking at him that Johnny was public school educated or one of the wealthiest men in the county. He wore old plaid shirts with frayed collars and a disreputable pair of moleskin trousers on which the zip fly was long-since broken. He had a pot belly which helped disguise the embarrassing fissure in the crotch area. Depending on the weather, his feet were clad either in walking boots or – more likely – ancient wellingtons with an arthritic big toe sticking through a hole cut for the purpose.

Johnny worked hard. As well as crops he kept a leading herd of pedigree Herefords and was renowned throughout the country for providing top breeding stock. He'd even sold bull semen to Australia, Argentina and the US. Unlike many farmers in his position, he didn't just drive around his estate in a Range Rover, monitoring progress and his team of workers; he got down and did whatever he could himself. He never delegated the dirty jobs, just got on with them. Consequently, he was not seen much in the village and few people knew him well. He avoided church (too busy) and the pub (ditto) but occasionally made forays to the village shop and Post Office, run by Mavis Hawkins.

Now, Mavis too was queen of her own estate although it didn't run to the sort of levels that Johnny's did. In fact, it must have been one of the smallest shops in the country, made even smaller by the fact that it was stocked to the gunnels. There was not only food and drink, sweets and cigarettes, but sewing requisites, gardening necessities, oddments of clothing, coal scuttles, children's toys, baby items, pet foods and accessories, hardware, electrical accessories, fishing tackle, bags of coal, wheelbarrows, veterinary supplies and goodness knows what else hidden from view. She carried more stock than the local town's supermarket and DIY stores combined – if she could only find it.

Mavis could never say 'no'. If someone – even a stranger asked for something she couldn't find or didn't have, she'd order a stock in on the basis that 'there was a demand for it'. She didn't take a deposit or even undertake to order it for the customer, she'd just get it in. Consequently, not only the shop but her whole house and even the garden shed were full of items that she'd perceived a demand for.

These included series of magazines from twenty years ago featuring characters from *Dynasty* and *Blake's 7*, spare parts for twin tub washing machines, packets of vegetable seeds with a 'best before' date of some 16 years ago, and a selection of music cassettes, floppy disks and a video library featuring early 1990s films. There was a garden roller in the downstairs loo, a large self-service dispenser of incontinence pads in her sitting room, and six galvanised dustbins in her bedroom.

Mavis did not own a computer, nor had she ever heard of eBay otherwise with some effort she might have cleaned up not only her property but converted much of the accumulated junk into a black bank balance.

Mavis's husband had died some years ago and it was following his demise that the levels of stock began accumulating. Alf had no interest in the world of retail but instead spent most of his time on his allotment. He justified this by displaying a sorry array of home-grown fruit and veg in front of the shop but most of the wireworm-infested potatoes and distorted carrots failed to attract any interest and ended up quietly being given away by Mavis.

I was in the shop one Thursday, carefully selecting my shopping. Mavis wore thick-lensed spectacles but even so, her sight was limited. It paid to shop slowly, examining each item's sell-by date and likelihood of inflicting food poisoning. I had bread and milk and was inspecting a pack of bacon when Johnny strode in.

'Morning Johnny', I said, 'enjoying this warm weather?'

'Oh, er, hello. Yes, er no, not really. It's too humid. Need the rain.' He looked around furtively.

Mavis had a soft spot for the farmer, especially since his too-posh-for-her-own-good wife, Portia, had cleared off with the children and abandoned him for a wealthy banker-type.

'Now, what can I get you, Johnny?'

I had been in the shop for 10 minutes and had been ignored!

'Oh, yes, thank you. Now, there was something.' He paused in deep thought. Then a sudden wave of relief came over him. 'Ah, yes. A letter here. Needs to go recorded. The ministry you know.'

'Well, I'll sort it out for you. Come over to the post counter. That envelope looks mucky, Johnny – wouldn't you like a new one?'

'I dropped it as I was coming through the yard.'

I could see that they were completely tied up in their transactions, so I continued my examination of labels.

'I think a nice azure envelope would be more fitting than that old manila one, don't you?' Mavis may have had little business sense, but you had to admire her selling techniques. Before Johnny could respond, Mavis had deftly found a pack of Basildon Bond envelopes and removed one whilst passing the remainder into Johnny's grasp.

'Write out the address details onto the envelope and transfer the contents while I sort out the Recorded Delivery.'

Johnny did exactly as he was instructed, and I continued shopping as silence descended for a few minutes. I was now checking a carton of eggs, but being from a local farm, there was no date of any sort on them. Dare I risk it?

Johnny finished and slid the new envelope under the grille to Mavis. There was a brief thank you before a rubber stamp was banged down expertly three times and she slipped a receipt back across the counter. Johnny paid the sum demanded.

'There you are – that'll be in Whitehall first thing tomorrow!' Johnny mumbled his thanks. 'Was there anything else I can get you?' she asked as Johnny struggled to stuff the remaining envelopes into his trouser pocket. I caught him looking across to see if I was listening. I turned my attention to a packet of tea, my ears straining to hear what might be said next.

'Err,' I caught him glancing across at me again. 'Err, I don't think... No, it's OK. I'll have to go into town anyway.'

He turned to leave. Mavis wasn't about to let a potential sale move off so easily.

'We stock more than you can see. What are you looking for?'

Johnny looked uncomfortable. He stared at the floor, halfway to his escape. Eventually, his manners asserted themselves and he turned back to the counter, but he still couldn't look Mavis in the eye. 'Err.... It's not easy. You see... I've never had to buy them before...' His voice trailed away. Mavis could see a sale escaping. I had spent three minutes examining a packet of PG Tips.

'Come on, Johnny. You can ask me!' Mavis glanced across as if only just noticing my presence. 'Would like to come to the back?'

'Oh, no,' Johnny blurted out as a fly might on being invited into a spider's web. 'It's... I can't even remember what they're called. Ladies' things. You know!'

Mavis was silenced for once. 'Ladies'things?' she retorted. 'Do you mean tights?'

Johnny regretted not having made his escape earlier. 'Not tights. You know... towels – that sort of thing.'

Mavis was visibly shocked. 'Have you got a new lady friend?' she demanded before her salesmanship reasserted itself. 'Sorry, it's none of my business. Is it Lil-lets you're after?'

Johnny was by now in agonies of embarrassment, his cheeks glowing bright pink. 'I don't know! I don't know the difference. It's ones that go up if that makes sense...' He couldn't look at anyone.

Mavis stood straight as a headmistress looking down her nose. 'You mean tampons!' she said in a much louder voice for my benefit.

'Yes, yes, that's what I need. Please can I just have a box, that's all I want. And large please.'

'A box? Yes of course. A heavy period she's having then?'

'What? No. There's no woman – had enough of that. No, I've got a cow with a discharge. The cowman says it's what she needs. It'd be much easier to just go into town and go to a self-service place.'

'Well, that's as maybe. But you don't get a personal service in them places. Do you?'

Richard Lutwyche

73

VHF Possibilities

Come in, Come in, Tin Tin
Tin Tin, Tin Tin, Tin Tack Tin
Tin, Tin Tin, Tin Tack
Tin Tack, Tin Tack,
Blue Tack
Blue Tack, Tin Tack, up one and hold?
...... hold
Get a Life, Get a Life, Lazybones
Lazybones, Get a Life, pick a channel,
Lazybones, Lazybones, Whalebones,
Whalebones
Whalebones, Turtlebones
Anybody got a trombone?

Dear Bridget, Dear Bridget, UR My Darling, UR My Darling
UR My Darling, Dear Bridget, ... allons soixante neuf?
Peakes stand by on six nine
OK, go...
Bottoms Up, Bottoms Up, My Lady Love
Whatever, Whatever, Mischief
Follow Me, Follow Me, Easy Lady
Why not, Why not, Why not

Sweet Music, Wild Thing
Ooh..., go..., Sweet..., Wild..., ...Over, Whatever...,
going up, Stand by..., ...going down...Darling,
Hold, ...come back, Come in please, That's a
roger, Ooh la la..., Again, ...and wait, Wherever,
Whenever, However, Mm, Mm, Mood Inde...,
Go, In, ...Out, In..., you're breaking up, come...,
Ooh..., U2?
Sweet Music, Sweet Music, Wild Thing
Wild

Kiss Me Kate, Kiss Me Kate, this is Red Devil, Red Devil
Kiss Me Kate
In Your Dreams, In Your Dreams, Shark
Farewell, Farewell,
Out.

This poem is a play on the names of yachts and VHF radio Etiquette.

Bridget Arregger

Why I write

'For as long as I can remember, I have enjoyed writing, whether diary, stories, letters to newspapers, word puzzles or teaching material. I am always writing something, whether in my head or on paper. I read. I argue. I write. It's nice when someone else likes it too.'

Essential Journey?

A poem for lockdown

Dual carriageway
empty in brilliant sunshine
frighteningly weird.
Me and Ian Dury on essential duty
to pick up garden bark.

Now we've time to fix things,
improve our life with a nice garden.

But there's no shopping.
Order everything from the nearest store;
drive, queue and wait at two metre spaces
alone.
Except for Ian Dury.

In the queue,
watch and wonder what they're doing here?
Is their trip essential?
Key workers?
or simply after garden bark?

Suspicion rife, we keep our spacing
Not because we're told to:
because we are afraid.

I journey home relieved
boot bursting with bags of bark.

Reasons to be cheerful?

May get a nice garden:
may live to see it bloom.

Dave Walklett

6. TERRITORY

'I COULD NOT DEEM THESE PLANETARY FORCES
ANNULLED
BUT SUFFERED AN EXCHANGE OF TERRITORY
OR WORLD'

EMILY DICKINSON

'The Highway of Death'

Audio

Birds glide south, on winds that rise
above Al-Jahra Plain.
With summer lost to the Earth's tilt chill
and autumn's hurry-up rain.
Each pass of time, a pendulum's swing,
each beat a repeat of the eagle's wing.

A Caravan trod north on sands that clothe
the vast Al-Jahra Plain,
its season lost to men possessed,
and those who would avenge... again... And now,
each bird that passed was a man-made thing,
each olive dropped came with a sting.

The travellers heard those silver birds
scouring Al-Jahra Plain;
whose screech announced that after all,
the day, for them, would end in pain.
Each flight of birds was a godless whim,
each mission flown with a devil's grin.

Napalm fixed, scorched skulls smile wide,
set within Al-Jahra Plain;
as feathered birds soar up, and up,
their preferred height to gain.
A fond 'God Bless!' the smiles suggest,
to the birds' transition at Times' behest... and yet...

In times gone by I'd stood there, in a culvert, gazing up,
as eagles flew high, their course sustained,
by the winds of Al-Jahra Plain.
A spiral flight on thermals tight,
they'd vanish at great height...
And I was privileged to see that sight... But now...?

The man-made birds, with stoops so brief, have changed
my fond memories into tableaux of grief... Yet, still...

Birds glide south, on winds that rise
above Al-Jahra Plain.
Their summer lost to the Earth's tilt chill
and autumn's hurry-up rain.

Selwyn Morgan

In the spring of 1991, a convoy of vehicles containing fleeing Iraqi soldiers and Iraqi civilians was attacked by US military aircraft. The action was described by military analysts as a 'Turkey-shoot'. Over 2000 soldiers and civilians died in the attack. The road, led from Kuwait City to the border with Iraq. Highway 80 has subsequently become known as the 'Highway of Death'.

From Ploughshare to Seaxe
The Battle of Stamford Bridge 1066

In three weeks, in 1066, a Saxon army fought three battles. The army was made up largely of farmers who laid down their ploughshare and took up their 'seaxe', a short sword favoured by Saxons. These farmer-soldiers joined the army in the south and marched over 200 miles to York; and then, after two weeks, over 250 miles to Hastings.

'Lanferth, Lanferth! It is you; by the holy mother of God, I thought that giant had killed you when he swung his mighty Dane Axe; I saw you falling into the river, your blood gushing, and then lost to sight in the melee as we charged the bridge... Are you all right? Tell me, are you all right?'

'Beorhtweard, Beorhtweard, yes it's me' Lanferth whispered, through the fog of pain and the congealed blood covering his face.

'And yes, you did see blood. I swear on the name of our Holy Saviour, it was the Viking's blood mingled with mine. He had killed forty or more of our brave warriors trying to get across the river.'

Lanferth paused, living again for a brief moment, that battle within a battle, tears in his eyes.

'Our good friend, Eadhelm the Woodcutter was amongst the bravest. He made the first rush at that giant, yelling and swearing on the relics of the saints. He fell with one swift blow of that axe. We must find his body and make sure he gets a hero's burial.'

'Lanferth, *you* are alive; bloodied but alive.'

'Yes, more than can be said of that Norse giant, a hero himself of his warrior clan, holding us at bay for so long... Yes, you saw me, but not falling from the bridge. I was coming up at that hero from below the bridge. I had straddled a log, and with my shield as a paddle, reached the middle of the river. That giant, tiring of his deadly exertions, did not see me in the confusion of the battle'.

Lanferth was weak; he paused and asked Beorhtweard for a drink from his flask. He drank slowly, with gasps and gulps. Beorhtweard used the water also to wash away the congealed blood of the deep cut across Lanferth's scalp.

'I was under the giant, and seeing my opportunity, I forced my war-shaft between the boards and pierced him in his belly. It was a mortal wound, but he did not die immediately. He fell over the parapet and struck out at me, our blood mingling as he hit the water. I finished him off, using my seaxe to deal the fatal wound.'

'As his body disappeared under the water, I thought of his courage and strength; I prayed that he would join the heroes in the mead hall of his ancestors'

Beorhtweard was silent for a few minutes, taking in what his friend had just told him. 'You also are a hero, a brave and true warrior. Our people, in the farms and villages of the Valley of The Meon, in far-away Wessex, will mourn our dead heroes and offer garlands and a feast on our return to the valley. Your story, and that of the Norse hero, will be told by our children and their children in great halls across the land. "Lanferth, son of Beowulf, and the Viking warrior, a true and worthy son of Grendel!"'

Lanferth slowly pulled himself up into a seated position. He could hardly believe what he saw, bodies and weapons of the fallen, as far as he could see.

The battle had started mid-morning. It was now dusk; the fighting had ceased. Saxon warriors were crossing over the bridge, wounded, exhausted, friends lost, but not defeated.

As Lanferth's head began to clear, it filled with the cries of dying men coming from the hill across the river. He thought,

What has happened to our leader, Harold Godwinson and his two loyal brothers Leofwyne and Gyrth..? How many of our country men would not again see their farms and families..? What about Tostig, Harold's brother, who had joined Harald Hardrada of Norway and his Norse army..? How many of these would-be invaders had been cut down..? How many would be returning to their boats? Exhausted, wounded, our warrior-farmers divesting their heavy, ragged tunics, laying down bloodied weapons and shields...

Night fell, the talk around the campfire was of friends who had fallen on this, the bloody feast of Ceolfrid and Egelred; and of families, missed, waiting, not knowing.

Mead flowed freely until these thoughts of home and loved ones beckoned the light of the dawn.

Peter O'Sullivan

Audio

Biography

Why I write

'Barely a blink of an eye, in a universe of infinite time. But for me it is me; my life, my touching, being touched. Memories experienced by many, unique to me. Anticipating, surprised, fun-loving, in-love, shocked. Memories to capture, to share, to learn, to re-live, to enjoy and not to fear. That's Why I write.'

Wild Honey   *Audio*

A spider's web spun across Nepali cliffs
And the white monkey's hand
Reaching down for his
Shows his inheritance as surely as the shaman said.
The long ropes
Woven from bamboo
The intricate knots on each step
To prevent side-slip.

The father tells the boy his dream is
Portent - it's how his life will be.
Clumsy at school, his classmates call him weak.
But Rongkemi spirit flames
His soul.
At 15 the first climb proves him a man.

A cold stone warning in his gut
when his first wife dies.
But he waits in calm
'Til the rhododendrons cover the mountainside,
the ripening season, and the journey begins.
Two days through dense jungle, discarded shoes
and quickening night,
the fire quenched at dawn.
Three sacrificial hens a blood memory.
Whilst he drank deep from the gourd.

Filtering light
Brightens as the canopy recedes.
They navigate in the sound of a crashing waterfall
The icy river
where now his feet clutch slippery stones.
The Tanje hunters
Move forward inexorably.

Above the clouds, spirits watch
Wild honeybees unwilling to leave their nests
Parted by smoke and incense
Of burning leaves
Three hundred feet below.

Step by step the beckoning cliffs.
Machete and mask
his only aid.
Up and up
And sheer,

Near the top an overhang
The ladder outswings
in mid-air.

Far below his shouts were heard
And pulleys on the collecting basket
Stay the spin.
His heart is beating fast
No monkey hand to reach for
And everywhere stung by angry bees
His face, his hands, his eyes.

See the hexagonal stickiness
Worlds he will desecrate.
Hallucinogenic honey dripping from his hands.
Scooped into the basket
In a funnel of noise
Pivoting in the slipstream
Of fury.

No successor can be found
After his hunting years are spent.
The bees and traders long gone
And the tribes unwilling

To be a spectacle.
The last of their kind.

Clare Finnimore

Biography

Why I write

'I write because I like words and what they can convey, and I'm on a high if I get it right!'

No Small Thing

Come, Dafydd, let's sit here next to Iolo. Cwtch up to me as the setting sun warms our backs and the wind blows in our faces. Do you hear it whispering songs as it carries the voices of the valleys across the ocean? Listen to the calls of the birds as they swoop and glide on its currents. They are plaintive, insistent, as if they are calling us home.

It's not too late to go back. At least, that's what Mam says in her letter. It only arrived this morning. *There'll always be a home for you and Dai Bach here. This is where you belong,* she says. We always used to call you Dai Bach, Dafydd. Mam still does. You'll always be Dai Bach to her, Little Dai, a babe who has only just learnt to crawl, still the same as you were the last time she saw you. But for me, you stopped being Dai Bach when we got off the ship and heard the news. Iolo, my young, strong, vital lover, was dead. It was at that moment you stood up, held onto my hand and took your first faltering steps. It was as if you knew you were the man of the family now, and so you became Dafydd.

But perhaps this evening, since we are talking of the past, you can be Dai Bach one last time, while I tell you the story of how we came here to this dry, dusty place from the rain-washed valleys of Wales and why we are sitting next to the grave of your father, my husband. Do you see what's written on his headstone? *Out of the strong came forth sweetness.* That's from the *Bible*, Dai Bach.

It was four years ago Iolo sailed on the *Mimosa*, the tea clipper that brought the very first settlers to this place. They had been promised a land flowing with milk and honey. Instead, they found a wasteland, parched and barren. There were over a hundred and fifty people in the party: teachers, scholars, clerks, preachers. Men, whose tools were words, paper, pen. Some came with their wives and children. Only

Iolo, with his miner's skills, and Gwyn Edwards, a farmer, knew how to wield the axe and till the ground.

Iolo took the lead and organised the men, and women too, into digging channels into the hard rock to irrigate the land, then Gwyn oversaw the planting of crops. They scarred their hands and almost broke their backs as they toiled in the hot, arid desert.

When the first growth appeared, Iolo sent for us.

Mam didn't want us to leave.

'What do you want to go to Patagonia for? We'll have Dai Bach growing up a heathen.'

'He won't grow up a heathen,' said Dad. 'Not with the Reverend Jones in charge. You know what Iolo said in his letter – they're already building a chapel.'

Dad organised my travel, hiring Elwyn Pony to take me to the station. There's grand it was to sit up on the trap with you on my knee as Elwyn Pony urged his old mare on. Queen Victoria herself could not have had a better send-off. The whole village lined the streets as they waved us goodbye. But sadness with it, for I would never see Mam and Dad again. It's no small thing to leave your old life behind and travel thousands of miles to a new world.

Perhaps when you are a man grown you will cross the stormy seas to visit the old country where you were born. You are like Iolo, Dai Bach. There's a restlessness in your spirit and tempest in your eyes. You need a man's steady hand to guide you as you grow to manhood and for me, well, a woman needs a man, especially in this hostile land.

Tomorrow I will have a new husband and I will be Mrs William Jenkins. Will's a good man, Dai Bach, and gentle in his courting. It's no small thing to wed a grieving widow and care for another man's son. He'll be a fine father to you.

But that is for tomorrow. Tonight as the sun sinks behind us we will sit and look across the land where the green shoots are piercing through the once barren soil. That's Iolo's work, Dai Bach. Out of the stone he brought forth growth. That's no small thing.

Iris Anne Lewis

Carol

Audio

Snow in desolate abundance

The village is hushed
and waiting

Helmeted in ice, three graveyard
yews stand on guard

Inside the church, a crusader lies
entombed in stone

Candles light a crib and
swaddled child

By his side a sword,
tipped with blood

Bright as a holly

Iris Anne Lewis

First published in The High Window 2020.

Biography

Why I write

'Writing, for me, involves exploration, expression and communication. Researching a topic or an experience is an enjoyable part of my writing process. I also love exploring the possibilities of language in my writing and take care to consider the sounds, meanings and associations of individual words and phrases when composing my work.'

Patinage

Audio

A fragile girl
In frail attire,
Escorted by her prince,
Steps out upon a chilly sea of glass,
Transformed from human
Into airborne mayfly
At a glance.

And as the music swells
They swirl and glide
Like magic
On a silver thread of steel,
No longer man and girl
But butterflies entranced
Swooping, spinning, twirling
In heart-stopping traceries
Of acrobatic flight,
Defying gravity,
Balanced on one blade
At agonizing speed.

And then he throws her
Like gossamer,
Spinning threefold –
Impossible, it seems,
Yet artful in extreme.

Without a blink,
She lands one footed,
Still sailing on,
Unbroken thread
Of motion....
And what, I wonder,
What impossibilities
Would she dream that night?

And then, triumphant pose,
Hands held aloft, it ends,
And, gliding swans transformed,
They waddle on dry land
Mere man and maid, once more.

Linda Dyson

Biography

Why I write

'I have loved writing since composing my first poem about hollyhocks at the age of seven and writing the opening chapters of a "novel" in an exercise book aged nine. I haven't really stopped since despite, or perhaps because of, a varied life spent in several countries.'

Cargo

Tap, tap, tap.
Milo climbs the final stairs, legs aching, ears cocked, determined to locate the source of the noise.
Tap, taptaptap, tap, tap.
He'd woken at 6am, crazy early as Grandpa would say, the distant sounds like fingers tapping on the inside of his head.
'Can you hear that?' he'd asked at breakfast.
'Hear what?' Grandpa said, from behind his newspaper.
'Eat your breakfast.' said Mother, who was soon gone to whatever she did in the city, leaving him to Grandpa. Who was soon fast asleep, leaving him to explore.

Tap, tap, TAP, tap.

Milo has run out of stairs, of breath. Before him stands the final attic door, right at the top of the rattlesome building, a room he has never entered. Milo reaches for the handle, which should be locked.

But isn't.

Inside, Milo forgets the unlocked door. A flock, a school, a squadron of coloured balloons jostle and squeak outside the vast attic window.

TAP, TAP, TAP, TAP.

The balloons carry ballast, small items which tap against the glass. Odd things: lengths of bone, pencil sharpeners. A battery, a pen. Each tied to its respective balloon with string, thread, even ribbon.

Each balloon also carries a scrap of ragged paper.

Within seconds Milo has opened the window, scooped them inside and begun investigating. Each scrap of paper bears a drawing, small but intriguing. And somehow two hours have passed and Grandpa is calling him for lunch.

As he leaves, Milo looks back through the window. In the far distance upwind lies a dark smudge on the landscape. The Camp, notorious from the TV news. Filled with refugees from the East. Half-savages, wild people, invaders.

'Grandpa! Look what I *found!*'

Milo will never forgive Grandpa for squealing on him.

He stares out of his bedroom window, lip wobbling. Below, Grandpa feeds the scraps of paper, the punctured balloons, even the ballast into the flames of a brazier as Mother watches.

She has been quite specific. The attic is now firmly locked and strictly out of bounds. The Camp is not to be discussed.

Milo has been hearing about it and its occupants for as long as he can remember. People driven from their homes by conflict, come West in search of... anything. Food, water, a roof over their heads, a chance of survival. A future. They have no money, and can't work.

'They contribute nothing to society.'

Milo remembers the pictures on the scraps of paper, the scribbled words in their foreign script. He loves to draw, but he has never managed anything so beautiful; he feels shame that his first reaction to them had been envy. Now he just misses them, wonders about their creator, imagining some small exotic person, clutching a pencil, somewhere in the distant Camp.

Can they all draw? He wonders. And wakes at dawn to a disappointment of birdsong.

The drawings were so beautiful. Animals and birds and boats and cars and things he doesn't recognise but yearns to know more about. Caught so easily, so deftly, on scraps of paper torn from books and newspapers. So flammable.

His mother's books, Grandpa's newspapers, sawdust from the rabbit hutch. Matches from the kitchen.

Mother is at work, Grandpa asleep, Milo has plenty of time. He soon finds the key to the attic in Grandma's purse, tucked away in a wardrobe.

Back up in the forbidden attic Milo stares out at the Camp, barely visible through the rain. He steels himself and the fire is soon lit, just as Grandpa taught him, on an ancient breadboard that nobody will miss. The attic is soon bright, he hopes the flames will be enough, that he has enough fuel to keep it going, that it will serve its purpose. An hour passes. Milo makes three trips downstairs for fuel, anything that will burn. Even his own drawings, those he is most proud of.

But it's getting late, the fire is dwindling and he is reluctant to take more risks. Grandpa will wake soon, his mother will return from work, his absence will be noticed.

And then he sees it, almost afraid to look in case it's his eyes playing tricks. Balloons approaching from the East. But not in ones and twos, to tap, tap, tap on the window. A cluster of balloons, all sharing the weight of a single cargo. A passenger, child-sized.

Milo hurries to open the window, already anticipating the first drawing they will make together.

Stephen Connolly

Originally selected for Stroud Short Stories 2018
and first published in Fictive Dream 2019.

Audio

Why I write

'I write to turn ideas into finished pieces and send them out into the world, to see them fly. To entertain, surprise, provoke. To make the reader think, laugh, engage. To hopefully give readers the same sensations and experiences I remember when I first read good pieces.'
www.stephenconnollywriter.com

Winter's Orbit

When winter came they left,
drawn by some horizon on an invisible path,
their deep prints cupping the shadows of the moon,
leaving cavernous messages,
a tracker's dream.

Above, the stars slow wheeled as land and sky fused,
up was down and down was up,
and the territory curled around
trapping them in winter's orbit.

Inside infinity they lost their ways
but fear of eternity drove them on
to prise the sky from the land,   *Audio*
to force another dawn.

Tina Baker

Women Exhibited

Audio

Here are the women,
written in the earth.
A fan of bones; vertebrae like corks,
their message delicately
inscribed by herringbone fingers.

At Kingshill North, her knees were bent tenderly to chest.
A warm slope and a red pot, honouring
a tooth-sore, bronze-age traveller.

And three thousand years away
in the next gallery,
her Anglo-Saxon sister
leaves traces of her
colours fossilised
in the corrosion
of metal objects.

Their speaking bones are whispering to us.

I see you.
I am listening,
you buried
and unburied
women.

Sophie Livingston

Entitled

Time stands still
Neglect startling
Rotting gates
It's history heartbreaking

Towering above
It's survived through the years
Standing majestic
Not for the poor

Wealth and status
Life divine?
No, not here
Lives shattered time after time

If walls could speak
The truth would astound
Nothing to envy
Best keep your feet firmly on the ground

Noni Bright

7. Time

'Time and Tide
Wait for no man'

Geoffrey Chaucer

The Serpent Ring

===

From minuet to jig.
Conceived in the union of separate parts
from affiliated passion, or single-minded rage
came the first born babe, mewing and a spewing
to commence its entropic dance, from a minuet to jig.
It trying to be different, yet condemned to be the same
whether winning battles pyrrhic or losing at life's game.
Building spoil heaps of its triumphs, or grave-pits
for its fame, each fractal of existence spawned
a fractal once again – from a minuet to jig.
Each spiral lost in the spiral whole, each
dance serene, until the final blow
turns a minuet to -

===

Selwyn Morgan

Audio

This poem, 'The Serpent Ring', is taken from the author's novel,
Going Up Camborne Hill, Amazon 2020.

Procession

Audio

The watchers are separate from them,
the pale ones, the distant ghosts,
a troop of white-suited soldiers
pressed to march to an unknown war.

No one knows what awaits them,
not even the onlookers,
crowding up to the unseen barrier
as they watch the ghosts shuffle by.

Do the ghosts see their faces,
catch their eyes, notice their friends,
look at their neighbours?
Or are they aware of nothing
but the smoke of the chimney,
the hidden blazing fires,
stoking up heat, pumping out smoke?

A towering cross divides the faceless
from the lifeless, the pallid from the living,
motionless in their muted coloured clothes
as the river of ghosts flows on.

A banner, cinder red, dark as coal,
billows like a sail behind the ghosts,
pushing them, driving them, forcing them
into the certain unknown.

Iris Anne Lewis

*An earlier version of this poem was published in The Blue
Gate Anthology 2014.*

Coat

An old, grey coat behind the door
shows signs of decay
like the carrier bag
in which the decaying old man
puts his decayed old socks
to be washed.

No-one washes for him.

Alone with his coat
and the photograph, crumpled and torn,
kept in his vest
he sleeps.

Some things are timeless:
an oak tree
or a hole in the road
left, forgotten.

People are momentary.
Even a photograph
recalls only a glimpse
of a loved one,
perhaps long gone.

So the old man dies;
another old man is born
and time hurries on
and waits for no man.

Dave Walklett

Biography

Why I write

'I write because I have stories
to tell and I am the only one
able to tell them, because they
are mine alone.'

A Hot Summer Day in Cougnac   *Audio*

The cave is cool and spacious.

I see a frieze: mammoths,
three megaloceros,
and two wounded men,
spears thrust in their sides.

Two red-coated pillars
of calcite frame
an ibex.

And I remember a hot summer day
when I took refuge
in a cool country church.

Pillars of fluted stone
framed a cross
and a wounded man,
his side gashed by a spear.
Above him, in stained glass,
a lamb.

And now, in Cougnac,
I look at the ibex
but see the Lamb.

Iris Anne Lewis

Highly commended, Bradford on Avon Arts Festival..
First published 2017 in
www.dawngorman.co.uk/words_and_ears_competitions.psp

COP26. A Shake Up Call?   *Audio*

Was it a dream,
a phenomenon of night?
A rumble, a flash, a beam of light?
Outside, nothing to see
Sleepwalking, wandering free?

I wake up, go outside, look around
'What's that black thing on the ground?'
Good Morning Britain is on TV
Covid, vaccines, usual bling

A news flash, is this the thing?
A fireball, from the cosmos far,
Winchcombe's very own star?
From far reaches of the distant sky
A meteorite has hit close by.

A sign, five billion years beyond
To shake us from our deep despond.
Is it a message, older than Earth?
From long before our planet's birth.

Just for us? No, it's for all.
A sign, a shake-up, no accidental fall.
Urgent! We have a choice
Death-or-life, with one voice.
Choose no action, death, nay-say?
Or embrace, love Earth, now! Today!

Peter O'Sullivan

Inspired by the 2021 UN Climate meeting and my thinking
a fragment of Winchcombe Meteorite landed in my garden.

Wedding Dress

Were someone to ask,
I wouldn't remember your dress,
though I remember the wedding.
I've seen photographs, of course,
but
I can't remember the dress.

You've worn it since, on stage
in My Fair Lady
and to parties where you wanted to impress.

And you did, as always.
But now
in a plastic bag,
behind the bedroom door, it gathers dust
and fades.

Dave Walklett

Out of Curiosity

Well known as a local artist, and with something of a reputation as a restorer, I have been given the task of cleaning some paintings in a pub. I take the first one home.

It's a big painting – almost two metres by a metre-and-a-half. It depicts a cow with river, hills and mountains in the background, and with grasses and ripe wheat in the foreground. It is a curious mixture of typical Victorian and something indefinably *not* Victorian.

The paint is darkened by a few years in the pub when smoking was allowed. It is surprising how dirty paintings get from smoke and beer. The back of the canvas is discoloured and stained and looks older than the ornate but cheap gilt frame that is stamped 'made in Taiwan'.

It is not valuable – not quite in the category of 'potboiler', but not authentic, and with poor brushstrokes. It is an amateurish attempt. It will not matter if I damage it. I could paint them a new and better one.

I remove the canvas from the frame and begin the initial stages of washing with warm water with a touch of ammonia to remove the superficial dirt, drying it with a soft cloth to prevent the water seeping into the canvas.

Then to remove the varnish. A scribbled note on the back of the frame tells me that unlike older paintings this has been finished with modern polymer removable varnish so this is a simple job of wiping with a slightly stronger solution of ammonia, section by section, so that the canvas does not become saturated. I open all the windows and endure the choking smell.

I stand back. The painting is now bright and light and looks freshly painted. That is probably all that is needed. I give it a second wiping with clean water and put it aside in sunlight to dry thoroughly and brighten still further, while I buy some new dammar varnish. This will give a slightly less glossy finish and sit better on the oil paint.

I turn the canvas over to deal with the back, carefully cleaning out the trapped dust. No cigarette butts or drawing pins. Or coins. But as I remove the last wedge, I see a tiny corner of paper peeping out from under the canvas. I fetch tweezers and gently draw it out. It is a brief love letter on computer printer paper, saying only,

'My love, I know how you adore cows. This young virginal heifer looks as if she has a secret to tell – she is soulful and curious about you. Are you curious about her?' L.V.

I turn back to the painting and notice there appears to be a red underpainting. Some of the red is revealed with each scratch and twist of a pointed stick that has been used to depict the stems of wheat. This is a technique I love but I think of it as being recently introduced, more recent than Victorian. Not only the varnish and frame are new.

I *Google* 'Victorian Cow Paintings' and find *The Craven Heifer* from a painting and engraving by *Fryer* and *Whessell* in 1811. The cow is almost identical but the background is significantly different. My curiosity now piqued, I buy a copy of the poster and lay them side by side. The poster is twenty inches by sixteen, about a quarter of the size of the canvas, and designed to fit standard frames.

The pub painting is not as skillfully painted. Nice technique with the red underpainting though. *That* does not appear in the poster. The scratching indicates some knowledge and skill on the part of the painter. He has probably used the end of his paintbrush. As someone has pointed out, 'You may as well use the hard point as well as the brush – you have paid for both ends'.

I pick away at the paint in the lower-left corner, gradually revealing the dark green plant of the poster version under the modern irises. I also find the hidden folly further up on the left. Was the artist worried about copyright even for a common painting like this? Or couldn't paint well enough? But why cover the original? It's well known and readily available as a poster. Why conceal the earlier one? Vanity perhaps. Wanting to pass off the painting as his own. Or her own. I look carefully at the signature. Initials only. *L.V.* Is that real? A code? A joke? Love? Lover? Elvie? Perhaps this modern artist is the writer of the love letter. Perhaps not. No clue to the identity or date, but recent, not Victorian. Someone practising painting? Using someone else's painting as a base? As I take off more paint, I find it is only a paper poster underneath. It has been blown up in sections from the original size, pasted on and painted over. Curiouser and curiouser. What is this amateur thinking of? Saving money? Picked up an old canvas in a junk shop? Pasted the print over it and painted over to make it his or her own? Wanting to impress the lover?

I stand back. There appears to be a pattern to the underpainting with variations in the red occurring in straight lines.

I pick away at the straight lines. Disappointingly, they are merely the joins in the sections of enlarged poster. I had half expected another letter, cunningly hidden in the thick paint. I stand back and survey the mess I have made of the cow. No going back now. If the pub owners want the cow, I shall have to honour my foolish boast and paint them one. What have I got to lose? Wild optimism, or meddlesomeness, prompts me to continue digging.

I'm not sure whether I am astonished or vindicated when, as I remove some of the paper, I find another layer of paint.

This is getting serious. I begin to photograph repeatedly as I start to remove the poster carefully, minuscule bit by minuscule bit, with a scalpel.

Parts of a further painting are gradually uncovered. It seems to be a very ugly scene of rape and hacking with swords and spears, with devils and monsters. No wonder our modern lover covered it over. I dread what I might find. I can't go on. I put it aside in horror.

That night, I dream of devils and angels. I wake with a strange sense of déjà vu. Of dread and despair mixed with hope and lightness. The painting is obscurely familiar so I have a closer look, and *Google* 'devil paintings'. I remove more of the poster and expose a poorly executed copy of a painting by Pieter Bruegel the Elder - *The Fall of the Rebel Angels* of 1562. There are some noticeable differences so this may be an earlier attempt by Breugel or, more likely, poor craftsmanship by the copier. As I lightly clean this of sticky paste and other grime and dirt, my cloth tells my fingertips there are more straight lines. Gently, I pick at the next layer of paint. This time I do find a letter buried in the pigment. This earlier artist has apparently painted thickly over Breugel's canvas to match the original as competently as possible and thus conceal the letter. However, that is not quite the case. The fine velour document tells of the dissolution of the monasteries during the reign of Henry VIII in the 1540s. A monk, perhaps, not a very skilled painter, but a clever one, has not only hidden the letter but copied over something he wanted to protect from the pillage of the monasteries by the king.

With the help of restorers more expert than me, we discover a rare, old, beautiful and extremely valuable painting - an early version of the striking and unusual *Virgin of the Rocks* by Leonardo da Vinci from about 1490.

The faces of the virgin and child are lit by sunshine and engender hope, in contrast to the dark, sombre rocks of the surroundings.

Bridget Arregger   *Audio*

'For Those in Peril on the Sea'

He has grown old as they that are left grow old. Motionless beneath a grey anorak and a tartan travel rug, he sits huddled against the November chill, small and bent in the wheelchair. The cub mistress, shepherding her young charges towards the memorial, draws them aside to allow his carer to manoeuvre him to the front of the small crowd.

Flanked by the bowler-hatted British Legion contingent, the bugler and the church choir are already in position. The hooded eyes under the flat cap focus on the only splashes of colour in the square, held loosely by dapper, blazered veterans, the eternal poppy wreaths. The clock on the tower shows 10.53.

That wind off the North Sea could cut you in two at HMS Royal Arthur, the Royal Navy shore training unit. The standing joke was how often German propaganda reported having sunk her. New recruits knew the elements were more likely to get them there than enemy action. Falling in on that 1941 morning with Charlie, Cyril and the rest of the crew, wet leaves from bare trees gusted round their feet and a fine rain fell. Five months in uniform and due to be posted, it was their first Armistice Day parade.

He could see Jean in the front row of the WRENS, as upright this morning as she'd been legless last night. He risked a wink as they marched past but she made no response. Madam, he thought, still playing hard to get – and they only had a few weeks left there. But he'd get her in the end.

With robes flapping in the wind, the vicar makes his way down the church path. The custom is to read aloud the names inscribed on the memorial, or rather on the list secreted in his pocket and for which he fishes as the crowd shuffles and coughs. The timing is crucial to get them in before the 11.00 o'clock signal. Old bugger never gets it right, he thinks, he'd never have done on torpedoes.

The Yanks were in by 42. He'd done nearly a year on North Atlantic convoys, knew the Eastern Seaboard like the back of his hand. They'd been very welcoming, knew how much the Brits had seen before they got in on the act. The Stella Polaris was in port on the 11th and they'd done church parade with the locals in clear, crisp New York sunshine. A family had asked them back to lunch afterwards – roast beef, apple pie, stuff you haven't seen for years, he wrote to Jean afterwards. Charlie had taken the daughter out a couple of times after that – nice kid with a ponytail and blue eyes. Damned if he could think of her name though. Probably the last girl Charlie ever took out.

He'd been lent to the USA requisition team for a month and was coming back across on another ship when some bastard U boat got them off Newfoundland. One of the best mates he'd ever had.

At the first stroke of 11.00, the crowd falls silent. Pushing off the tartan rug, he struggles to his feet.

It was tropical kit for Simonstown. They picked avocados in the orchards adjoining the camp and penguins strutted around them on Isopingu Beach when they played volleyball with the local kids. It was a joint services posting so the boys in blue and the army turned out with them too. They'd set up a drumhead altar on the parade ground and the young Scottish padre took the service in the full heat of the morning sun.

Two years down the line, he'd been promoted now. Married too, on a brief leave in Liverpool, both of them in uniform, no family but shipmates toasting them in brown ale in the Nelson's Arms. Put a different slant on things somehow. He felt it at that service. 'Hear us when we cry to Thee for those in peril on the sea' – and those poor sods flying the planes and driving the tanks and getting the living daylights bombed out of them at home.

The standards lower as the notes of The Last Post carry across the square. A tear, unbidden and unchecked, runs down his cheek.

He'd heard the news about Cyril when they were in port at Leith. So the poor devil would never know if the baby would play for Wales or grow up a cracker like her mother. He kept starting letters to the wife but they never sounded right. He thought about him a lot though in those mountainous seas around the Faroes. The Brimnes had done weeks on the Orkney / Faroes / Iceland run. Four hours on, four hours off on patrol but he never slept much. Even with all your kit on you never got warm and hanging on to the chains at either end of your bunk in the wireless room hardly made for restful slumbers.

On duty scanning the grey horizon, he caught glimpses of the brief service on the deck below. The skipper's words were lost in the crashing of the waves and the screeching of the seabirds but his shipmates standing to attention, saluting, standing at ease told him where they were in the familiar ritual. Glorious dead be buggered, he thought, let's get this whole shambles over and done with and get the hell out of it before any more of us sink without trace.

Reveille sounds. The carer takes his arm. She makes to restore him to the wheelchair but he makes no move. Age may have wearied and the years condemned but what has made him what he is has never left him. Jean would have understood. In the morning and at the going down of the sun – it's every day that he remembers them.

Gill Garrett

Audio

Winning entry Wootton Under Edge Arts Festival, short story 2012.

Why I write

'I write to make sense of the world I have lived in, the world I live in now and the world as I anticipate it will be - writing clarifies my thoughts, prompts me to question, to imagine, to reflect. It enables me to engage with a wide variety of people, to offer my perspective.'

8. GRIEF

'I MEASURE EVERY GRIEF
I MEET WITH NARROW, PROBING, EYES
I WONDER IF IT WEIGHS LIKE MINE
OR HAS AN EASIER SIZE.'

EMILY DICKINSON

Woodland Burial

Audio

A different type of pillow talk
we chose the plot together,
you rooted to the hospice bed
by tubes feeding opium sap.

You wanted oak and ash to
shelter you in broadleaved woods,
and in return to nurture them
with mouldered bone and flesh.

Tethered still to life, you slip into a
shadowed sleep. Death creeps closer,
steals your breath and shifts you to
a different state. I close your eyes.

Encased in willow, you now begin
your slow and secret work in deep
secluded dark, becoming one
with earth and plants and rain and sun.
Drifts of bluebells mark your spot.
Light, leaf-dappled, casts patterns on
your shaded grave. Bare branches arc
a latticed vault against the winter skies.

Iris Anne Lewis

*First published in Crossroads: Anthology for
Cheltenham Literature Festival 2015.*

Tagasode*

Audio

Whose sleeves?
Not yours, I hope,
on any canvas.
My gawky hands
could never ply the brush
to paint the pegs or frame
where your clothes would hang:
silk dresses, Kashmir scarves,
not needed any more.

My fingers would be grasping
at the air
you graced and moved until
the last breath left.

Frank McMahon

Tagasode: a frame where would hang clothes of a departed loved one, invoking memories.

First published in At the Storm's Edge, Palewell Press 2020.

After Lights Out

It's easy to blame Tony Foster. Almost everybody does. He threw the pitchfork.

But...

It was my idea in the first place and I would have gone on my own if they hadn't wanted to come too. It was already sunny and warm when we left the school at seven that July Friday morning to go swimming. We'd had special permission, five of us, to get up before the morning bell so we'd have an hour before breakfast.

For us it was just an adventure, a laugh. We'd show them. It wasn't totally spontaneous: we planned it a bit, whispering well into the night after lights out.

We had no intention of going swimming.

I'd been in trouble all week and was in trouble again. I'd had enough; running away seemed a solution. Seemed the only solution. Like I say, I would have gone alone: maybe I should have done.

By evening we'd hitchhiked sixty miles and needed somewhere to sleep. You could say the farmer was to blame. He showed us the barn full of hay bales and said it was ours for the night. He gave us cocoa and paraffin lamps.

'Can't have you wasting electricity!' he said, lighting the lamps. 'And you look like sensible boys.'

We put the electric light on anyway while we decided on sensible places to hang the lanterns.

As we prepared for sleep. I noticed Tony was quiet.

'What's the matter?'

'Rats!'

'What'

'There'll be a million rats in here. Always are in barns.'

'So?'

'I hate rats. They rip your throat out while your asleep.'

We sneered and sniggered and argued, but he wouldn't have it. Tony, who always reckoned he was such a hard man, was terrified.

I said, 'We can't sleep with this light on.'

'I'm not sleeping in the dark.'

I got ready to flick the switch. Tony picked up a pitchfork.

'You turn that off and I'll kill you!'

'You wouldn't dare.'

'Just try me.'

I turned out the electric light and Tony threw the pitchfork.

I'd been careful to put the door between me and him. I flicked the switch. I pushed the door shut.

The pitchfork hammered into the door and ricocheted off, knocking a paraffin lamp over on a bale of hay.

As I watched the flames swallow the barn and Peter Stuart, I wished we had gone swimming. I don't know why Pete didn't get out. When they found him they said it looked like he tripped or something. They said the whole thing, the fire and that, was just a tragic accident. You try telling Pete's mum that.

My mum was furious but at least she had me to be furious with.

We were taken back to school and caned.

We got a little bit of notoriety out of it back at school but I reckon I could have made so much more of this story if it hadn't turned out to be the only story I had to tell.

Dave Walklett

At the Storm's Edge

Audio

At the storm's edge
always, never knowing if it will discharge
and overwhelm, or if it will relent,
recede as the season drags itself upstairs and round the cot.
Or the days may reverse to that moment sundered
between joy and shock, the seconds scattered
across the antiseptic floor, silence drowning
the other's cry.

Light aches on the newborn's face
in the muffled house. A ghost demands
its feed, forever probing at the teat
with blue, waxed lips, growing thin on dreams.
At the storm's edge there is always a prayer.

The ghost is clothed, in a shoe-box laid,
carried away, an exit to be registered.

Frank McMahon

First published in At the Storm's Edge, Palewell Press 2020.

Inspired by the Haiku

rooks pairing
clamour swirling high
glide in the blue

our sacred river bed
women wade for lily roots
whitefellah show respect

passing the door quickly
I glimpsed her floating
no she's hanging

caught in your eyes
we disappear together
years to spend dreaming

an eyeball in the mud

kettle's steamy water
falls on ice
little beaks sip

autumn's suicide grey

talking around the fire
our human spirit
distilling into poetry

two old lovers exiled to Kyoto
sit in the marble hotel lobby

Norman Smith

Hannah

Audio

I'm reading poems to you this morning.
Me in my bookish space
Sunlight shining in from the east.

Yeats gives you Cloths of Heaven
treading softly on your dreams.

Christina Rossetti brings you Spring
in Dreamland.

If only you were here sweetheart
I'd be happy holding you.

Biography

Norman Smith

Why I write

'I capture fleeting thoughts and
moments.'

The Happiest Time of Year?

Audio

The happiest time for many,
but so difficult for some;
Our memories of past Christmases seem perfect.
So serene; rose-tinted I know!
But our darling Sam was with us then.

On Christmas morning, we open our presents.
In the afternoon, we walk to his grave and say the Lord's Prayer.
At dinnertime, I lay a place for him at the table
and even contemplate putting turkey on his plate.

But it's not till the evening,
when Dr Who (Sam's favourite) is shown;
that the relieving tears finally flow.
This is the fifth Christmas without our precious son.
But the pain is still so tender and so acutely raw.

Terasa Pilcher

Sam Pilcher

Innocence

We thought we knew
We thought we could have it all
If only we'd known
We didn't know
It could not be
Nothing can be forever

Terasa Pilcher

Why I write

'I have a very hectic and deman-
ding lifestyle, so writing is a rare
luxury. When an opportunity presents, it becomes a therapeutic
process that reminds me to make
more effort. Most of my writing
has been inspired by personal life
experiences, often sad, but I try to
inject humour where possible.
I constantly berate myself not to
procrastinate and to get writing!'

Diagnosis

Audio

The Consultant's Room
a gallery
exhibiting the scans,
my head
an apple sliced,
my core on public view.

To launch the show
an invited few
stand round, comment
on the pictures,
discuss design,
flaws in execution.

I have no trained eye
to appraise
the work of art.
My interest more visceral,
I await
their verdict.

Gill Garrett

First published in Tools of the Trade: Poems for New Doctors, Scottish Poetry Library 2015.

Postmortem

He eases the front door closed
on the last departing guest
turns
leans
listens to the silence.
Returns to the melancholy
to which he's become accustomed.

Forty-three years together
a mere moment:
a lifetime since she's gone.

When we retire
we'll move to a smaller house and
we'll buy a campervan
take a cruise
we'll lose our eyesight and our health
we'll watch each other die.

He eases the front door closed on the final mourning guest
and wonders what he will do
tomorrow.

Dave Walklett

Index of Members

Tina Baker

4	Childhood Clips
21	Within the Calm
55	The Compositor
97	Winter's Orbit

Noni Bright

99	Entitled

Linda Dyson

17	Sunset in the Golden Valley
92	Patinage

Graham Bruce Fletcher

18	Misheard Lyrics
24	Legacy
30	Bee or Not Bee
38	Tears
40	Familiarity
62	Dear Samuel Johnson

Clare Finnimore

54	Vermeer
85	Wild Honey

Iris Anne Lewis

2	I Shall Have to be Punished for Writing This
5	Cry of the Wolf
88	No Small Thing
90	Carol
103	Procession
106	A Hot Summer's Day in Cougnac
118	Woodland Burial

Sophie Livingston

19	Warm Day During the Covid-19 Lockdown
32	Louis the Painter
42	Origin of Species
43	Breathing Out
98	Women Exhibited

Index of Members continued

Frank McMahon

3	*Universal Credit*
10	*Sanatorium*
11	*Grace Notes*
16	*Wordsmiths*
50	*Playing Chess in a Steelworks*
119	*Tagasode*
122	*At the Storm's Edge*

Selwyn Morgan

51	*The Tin Miners*
59	*The Five-Cent Slots*
68	*Gobsmacked*
80	*Highway of Death*
102	*The Serpent Ring*

Peter O'Sullivan

82	*From Ploughshares to Seaxe*
107	*COP26, A Shake Up Call*

Clare Roberts

22	*River*
23	*Destination*
28	*A Better View*
39	*Cook*
61	*A Spree*

Norman Smith

123	*Inspired by the Haiku*
126	*Hannah*

Dave Walklett

20	*Some Haiku*
64	*Denis Kelly*
76	*Essential Journey*
104	*Coat*
108	*Wedding Dress*
120	*After Lights Out*
130	*Post Mortem*

Index of Past Members

Bridget Arregger

9	*Bull Steined!*
58	*Things to Do Every Day*
60	*Why I Don't Go Jogging Anymore*
74	*VHF Possibilities*
109	*Out of Curiosity*

Stephen Connolly

45	*Remember My Name*
94	*Cargo*

Gill Garrett

36	*Geography of a Love Affair*
48	*An Autistic Child*
113	*For Those in Peril on the Sea*
129	*Diagnosis*

Terasa Pilcher

127	*The Happiest Time of Year?*
128	*Innocence*

Richard Lutwyche

65	*Gudmundower's Soup*
70	*The Awkward Shopper*

Attribution of Photographic Images

1	Gas Mask	Danielle Tunstal	Pxb
5	Winter Chalet	Luca Chiandoni	
11	Tea and Biscuit	Kseniia Lopyreva	
15	Woodland Path	Frank McMahon	
24	Hoodie with Gun	Harrison Haines	
27	Baby Elephant	0ffd125gk87	Pxb
32	Rocky Shore	Ben Mack	
35	Violinist	Cottonbro	
38	Weeping Blood	Ferkanfdemir	
43	Injection	Karolina Grabowska	
45	Shopping	Furkanfdemir	
49	Cotton Mill	Tama66	Pxb
51	Trevithick Statue	Selwyn Morgan	
55	Wall Painting	Helena Ije	
57	Swings	Scott Webb	
63	Waste Paper	Steve Johnson	
65	Toadstool	David Waschbusch	
68	Piggy Bank	Cottonbro	
70	Milk Cows	Zak Halabie	
74	Two on Yacht	Yaroslav Shuraev	
	Man on Yacht	Sjostrom	
77	Car boot	Karolina Grabowska	
79	Fence and Flowers	Klimkin	Pxb
82	Berserker	Daniel H. Vicente	
88	Tea Clipper	Brigitte Werner	
94	Balloons	PhotoMix-Company	Pxb
101	Prague Clock	Anikinearthwalker	Pxb
109	Painter	Jean-Daniel Francoeur	
113	Sunken Ship	Marc Coenen	
117	Doll in Rocks	Counceling	Pxb
120	Schoolboy	Mikhail Nikov	

Printed in Great Britain
by Amazon

80953645R00081